Be the Life & Soul of the Party

Socialising for Success

Clare Walker

♛
Crown House Publishing Limited
www.crownhouse.co.uk

First published by

Crown House Publishing Ltd
Crown Buildings, Bancyfelin, Carmarthen, Wales, SA33 5ND, UK
www.crownhouse.co.uk

and

Crown House Publishing Company LLC
4 Berkeley Street, 1st Floor, Norwalk, CT 06850, USA
www.CHPUS.com

© Clare Walker 2000, 2005
© Illustrations Poppy Smith 2005

The right of Clare Walker to be identified as the author of this work has been asserted by her in accordance with the Copyright, Designs and Patents Act 1988.

First published in 2000 under the title *Socialising for Success: The Practical Guide to Perfecting Your Social Skills*. Revised and expanded edition published in 2005. Reprinted in 2006.

All rights reserved. Except as permitted under current legislation no part of this work may be photocopied, stored in a retrieval system, published, performed in public, adapted, broadcast, transmitted, recorded or reproduced in any form or by any means, without the prior permission of the copyright owners. Enquiries should be addressed to Crown House Publishing Limited.

British Library of Cataloguing-in-Publication Data
A catalogue entry for this book is available
from the British Library.

10 Digit ISBN 1904424996
13 Digit ISBN 978-190442499-4

Library of Congress Control Number 2005924701

Edited by Fiona Spencer Thomas

Printed and bound in the UK by
Cromwell Press
Trowbridge, Wiltshire

For Mum, with love and thanks

About the Author

Clare Walker is an NLP Master Practitioner and the founder of *Selfworks*. She originally trained as a barrister but now helps individuals and organisations enhance their communication skills. Having thoroughly enjoyed every social event she has been to for the past fifteen years, she has developed a unique system to allow others to do the same. Clare lives in London, UK, with her husband Jim.

Contents

Author's Note	ix
Introduction	1
Chapter One It's All About Attitude	15
Chapter Two Create Your Carrot	25
Chapter Three Everything But the Words	39
Chapter Four How to Talk About Anything	65
Chapter Five Questions, Questions	77
Chapter Six A Trip to the Theatre	85
Chapter Seven Get Ready …	101
Chapter Eight Get Set …	127
Chapter Nine Go!	137
Appendix 1 List of Activities	141
Appendix 2 Conversation Starters	143
Resource List	145

Author's Note

Author's notes are like Oscar speeches: best kept short. So I'd just like to say a heartfelt 'thank you' to everyone who made this book possible in whatever way ... long-suffering friends and family who've believed in me for so long, students, clients, colleagues, people who've made suggestions via the Web ... You know who you are and I'm hugely grateful.

Finally though, special thanks to Crown House Publishing for having the faith to publish *Be the Life & Soul of the Party* and to you for buying it. It's time to start the adventure. If you have any queries or comments about the book, or suggestions for the next edition, your feedback is always welcome. My contact details are at the end of the book. Whilst I can't promise an immediate answer, I will always do my very best to help if possible.

Have fun!

Clare Walker
London 2005

Introduction

Have you always wanted to be the life and soul of the party? Have you dreamt that the endless small talk could be transformed into a genuinely interesting event and that you could know, in your heart that it was you, at your very best that was holding everyone's attention, rather than the quality of the canapés? Better still, what would it be like if each party or event were an opportunity that led you one step further along the path that you really want to follow?

Or maybe you've always wondered how someone in your family or your workplace manages to know so many people or to get on in life so young, when you know far more than they do about your subject or have put in far more effort. Yet they are always talking, talking, talking, and succeeding. How do they do it?

You can learn to be the 'life and soul' of *any* party

The good news is, you can *learn* to be the 'life' and perhaps even more importantly, an important part of the 'soul' of every gathering from now on, if you choose to do so. It is a set of skills, a system, which is well within your grasp. Other people may, because of chance or circumstance, happen to use the right strategies naturally and, as a result, appear to be the life and soul of the party. The ideas in this book will enable you to approach all kinds of gatherings, from work events to weddings and dinners to dog-racing, with genuine confidence. What's more, as you have more fun at these events (and show it) so will the people around you. In turn, your enjoyment will create the conditions in which interesting opportunities can be presented to you and so create an upward spiral of ease and success.

You could be forgiven for cynicism here. How can the toe-curling embarrassment of meeting strangers be something that inspires excitement rather than dread?

Some people enjoy social events

The important thing to remember is that every person is different. No two people in the world, even identical twins, share the same belief systems, the same 'map' of reality. As the saying goes, 'one man's meat is another man's poison'. Therefore, just because you currently hold a particular view of partying or going to a workplace 'do', Christmas with the in-laws or similar, this is not necessarily the same as someone else's. Some people out there actively enjoy socialising with a purpose and even relish it just as much as gatherings with their 'ordinary' friends, because of the unique opportunities it presents. I know this, because, I confess, I am one of them.

More importantly, I've 'bottled this skill' into a form that I've seen works for people, across the board. I'll be sharing the stories of many of these people as we go along but, first of all, for those of you who like this kind of thing, here's how it all got started.

For several years, I never even realised that socialising was a skill. I wandered around (quite often enjoying seminars and dinners much more than my actual job) and was blissfully unaware that my more technically competent colleagues would have given their eye teeth to know how to charm their way into the next opportunity. Little did I realise that I had unconsciously set in motion a snowball, where the effects of my technique gathered momentum at each successive event and often continued to be felt for weeks, months or even years, into the future.

Everyone can learn new skills

It was only later when studying a branch of psychology that I became aware that getting on with other people and being the life and soul of the party, when appropriate, was a skill in itself. However, because it is a skill, it can be broken down into its component parts and taught to anyone else who wishes to learn. Skills are simply a combination of particular habits of thought, action and attitude, which, if they are linked together in a particular sequence, produce a desired result. This book will teach you to build and implement just such a sequence in relation to being the life and soul of the party.

Believe it or not, you have been learning such sequences throughout your life. Even when you learnt to walk, you needed a strategy. First, you grasped the furniture and stood. This taught you to balance but, even more importantly, it gave you the *belief* that you could balance. In turn, this gave you the confidence to make one tottering step, shift your weight on to that foot and step forward with the other foot. In that instant, you acquired the strategy for walking. Such was your unstoppable confidence after this mighty achievement (and the probable praise from your proud family) that the odd stumble, or even series of stumbles, did not then prevent you from perfecting the technique.

The only trouble is, you probably don't even remember that learning a new skill can and should be that simple. Most probably, as you've got older, you've suffered setbacks in certain situations that have led to nagging doubts, re-runs of previous embarrassing events and other self-criticism, which build up over time into a wall, needlessly holding you back. Therefore, this book explains the process of socialising from a much earlier stage than you might imagine. It begins with your beliefs, so that your self-confidence will be built upon a firm foundation.

Be the Life & Soul of the Party will then take you step-by-step through a process that will make the whole business of mingling with others at parties and social events more attractive. Specifically, the skills you'll learn here are:

- How to build a set of attitudes that support you in having more fun;
- How to create a vision of yourself having fun that will immediately make you want to start putting it into practice;
- Communication tips that work every time;
- Everything you need to consider in order to forward plan your ultimate triumph;
- Techniques to help you breeze through an actual event;
- The follow-up strategies that can make the rest of your life more fun.

What's more, the crucial follow-up phase that will ensure that your efforts (if you can really call something that's this much fun an effort) pave the way for future, as well as present, successes.

You already have the tools you need

Whether you are aware of it at the moment or not, you already possess all the skills you need to be the life and soul of the party. All you need to do is link together the resources and abilities you already have, in the right order and in the context of parties and social events. If you need further evidence, think for a moment about your everyday life. Unless you have lived permanently on a desert island, it is likely that at some point, you have already used some of the skills that will enable you to get on with others easily. If you have ever told a bedtime story to children, chatted on the phone to a friend or listened to someone else's tale of woe while waiting in a bus queue, then you have already been using the skills of someone who is the life and soul of the party.

What does being the 'life and soul' of the party mean anyway?

On one level, each of us has a different view about what it means to be the 'life and soul of the party'. For now though, here's what it means in relation to this book.

'Life'

First of all, it's about projecting 'life' into an environment that may need it by feeling confident enough to share a part of yourself with others. (The type of 'life' and 'sharing' will depend upon you.) I know of one person who used these ideas to move into cabaret and performance work but I also know a more academic person who was just delighted to be able to chat with his neighbours more easily. The choice is yours.

'Soul'

This is a key point that people tend to ignore. But think about it. Who is really showing more 'soul' and sharing more of themselves ... the roaring would-be extrovert who has to down a copious amount of booze and can-can on the table ... or someone who really listens to you, laughs and says and does what they find to be true about life in a way to which everyone can relate?

When is a party not just a party?

So, what kind of parties are we talking about? In short, any kind that *you* like and, while we're about it, please take the whole concept of 'party' as widely as you can. So the points in the system can be used at a gathering of any size, any place, anywhere, in just about any circumstances where there's going to be a conversation. (Let's face it, *How to be the Life & Soul of Conversations and Gatherings* just doesn't have the same ring to it as a title but it's how you can use these ideas if you so choose).

The important thing is that you use these ideas in the way that will be of most benefit to you and you'll only be limited by your imagination. For example, I had an email a few months ago from someone in New Zealand who was using these ideas to help secondary school children gain more confidence more quickly. Now I shall challenge you to be even more far-reaching in how and where you take these ideas.

Are there any limits?

Prepare yourself for a shock. Some people from the more saccharine end of the self-help scale will be horrified that I could even talk about limitations (after all, everything and anything's supposed to be possible, right?). However, limitations can be glorious and they focus your attention like nothing else.

Imagine if I'd said to you just then … 'No … go right ahead and apply any and every aspect of each paragraph in this book right across your whole life and do it as fast as you can, too.'

Well, I don't know about you but my reaction to that would be overwhelming panic and a fear of not knowing where to begin. So here's the deal. Yes, these techniques are hugely flexible and will work more-or-less anywhere but, in order to get them going in your life, especially at first, I'd like you to choose a particular way-of-being that you personally would like to have in a fairly well-defined situation. Then, as you get more confident and start to have more and more fun with these ideas, by all means apply them more widely.

What sort of situation should you explore to begin with? How specific do you have to be?

You, of course, can answer that question better than I. However, a good bet to begin with might be any kind of situation that a) immediately pops into your mind and/or b) you've wanted to feel *a lot* more comfortable about for a long time.

For example, one of my students always felt uncomfortable at weddings so worked with that. Another chose business conferences. It all depends on what you most want and need right now.

Above all, be yourself

One of the major themes of this book is the importance of being yourself as you approach others in any situation. Only if you are being yourself can you hope to be sincere. Other people will recognise your sincerity and respond to it accordingly with offers of help and unusual opportunities. The flip side of this concept also applies. If you act falsely and in a manner that is not in tune with your real personality, others will sense this and, quite unconsciously, withdraw slightly from your interaction.

The activities in this book are designed to ensure that, if you're truly honest with yourself, as you work through them, you'll be able to develop a style and 'way of being' with others that is comfortable and appropriate for you personally. You will not be required to become a great orator if you hate having to think of conversational topics. You will not be forced to wear red if you are wedded to brown. You will, however, be given the choice of a range of techniques that you can 'mix and match' to create a way of being that reflects all that is best in your real personality.

Neither will it be essential to follow each and every one of the pieces of advice on offer. Do what is comfortable for you. Take the example of my friend who hates Friday-night drinks. While she refuses to go to social events that make her feel uncomfortable, her workmates still adore her. Why? Because she is the person who brings in doughnuts every Monday morning. Now that's being the life and soul of a very welcome 'party' in its broadest sense.

What being the life and soul of the party means to you

Does this all sound too good to be true? If it does, think again about the phrase 'life and soul of the party'. What sort of thoughts spring to mind? Go through your thoughts, sense by sense and think about what you see, hear, feel, taste and touch in relation to being the 'life and soul of the party'. Don't forget to include any 'internal voices' that give you other subtle information. Write down your thoughts in the space below or on a separate piece of paper. Just write down whatever comes into your mind without judging it and, as with all the activities in this book, be as honest with yourself as possible. The exercises are designed for you to use by yourself so, by answering them as honestly as possible, you give yourself the greatest possible chance of success. When you are ready, carry on and read the next paragraph.

For me, being the life and soul of the party means …

_____

_____

_____

Does the idea of being the life and soul of the party make you feel positive and alive? Do you immediately see a bright picture of happy, laughing people in your mind's eye? Do you hear them responding positively to your contributions or do you immediately think of blank faces, a lack of communication and the idea that 'No one wants to talk to me'?

The chances are that, if you are interested in improving how you get on with and come across to others, the impressions you give tend more towards the negative than the positive. Can you see how you are in fact choosing your attitude towards parties and events? It may now be easier to grasp how by reading this book you will acquire the tools you need to make changes, if that's what you want.

Remember, this 'life and soul' business is a process

You will be able to achieve this success if you bear in mind two factors. First, the process is explained in small easy-to-follow chunks, almost like 'colouring by numbers', until you have made the process your own. Second, you need to remember that is indeed a *process*. It begins long before a particular event and continues long after it, sometimes for many years. That is why only one of the next nine chapters deals with approaching any one particular event.

Intention is everything

It might be that your thoughts about a single social event were quite positive and yet you still do not yet enjoy the idea of being the life and soul of the party. In which case, you might also be making some bigger generalisations quite unwittingly. Perhaps, for example, you automatically make a connection between 'life and soul', 'pushy', ' too loud' or 'rude'. This might indicate a negative belief that is holding you back needlessly.

In fact, this 'life and soul' process is completely neutral. Rather like the Internet, it can be used positively or negatively, according to the intentions of the user. Therefore, if you employ the techniques in this book with the intention of manipulating others, then that is the result you will achieve. If, however, you honestly wish to improve your ability to connect with others on a heartfelt level, then that will be your result.

Beliefs

However, before you can implement a successful socialising strategy, you need to understand your thinking at this moment. The activity above will have helped you to find out whether your view of being the life and soul of the party is broadly positive or negative. The next chapter will help you explore the beliefs that create your view.

How to get the greatest benefit

However you use this book, it will benefit you. Perhaps unsurprisingly, the more of the activities within it you carry out and continue to practise, the greater and more rapid those benefits will be.

Having said that, going to parties and events is an enjoyable activity (yes, really, it is). Therefore, it would be bizarre if the do-it-yourself kit here required you to feel that hours of arduous effort were required. Instead, get into the mood by thinking about just how much you will enjoy the process and how easily it will unfold.

It's also important that you think about what enjoyment means for you personally and tailor your approach to give yourself the maximum amount of *fun*. For example, some of the exercises suggest that you might like to record your progress in a notebook. If, however, you dislike writing things down and know full well that you'll never look at a notebook entry again, don't bother. On the other hand, some people like to have a tangible record of their progress and they will make copious notes. Similarly, certain people will complete various parts of the book more quickly than others. Your pace is your own and, as long as you follow the patterns given and the order in which they are presented, you should allow yourself to approach the activities in the way that suits you best.

Now, all that remains is for you to begin to enjoy the events that are about to unfold.

Imagining yourself as the 'life and soul' of a party

1. How would you define what you most want from this book?

_____

_____

_____

_____

_____

_____

If this definition contains any negative terms, (e.g. 'I don't want to be shy') rephrase it positively in the space below:

_____
_____
_____
_____
_____

2. What would an outside observer see, hear and possibly feel you doing in order to be able to agree that you have achieved that result (e.g. 'They'd see me being the first to strike up a conversation')?

_____
_____
_____
_____
_____

3. This may seem like a strange request but, next, please note down the benefits of your current reluctance to get this result. (To give you an example of this, one client found that ducking out of events gave her more time to study for her exams.)

_____
_____
_____

4. For each of the benefits listed above, think of a way to incorporate them into your new goal. (The client mentioned above limited her attendance to a given number of social events each week until she had passed her exams.)

_____
_____
_____
_____
_____

5. Make notes below of any occasions at which you would not like to socialise. Again, this may sound odd but I know that one of my own major problems (in an office environment) was to be *too* sociable, which severely limited my work rate.

_____
_____
_____
_____
_____

Check that you have the necessary time, energy, money and other resources (such as child care). If this is in doubt, focus on choosing the most time-efficient and cost-effective solutions in the rest of this book. If you feel comfortable with each of these steps, carry on to the next chapter. If not, repeat the above steps as many times as you need to in order to feel comfortable.

Chapter One

It's All About Attitude

It was one of my best friends who made me realise that being the life and soul of the party is a skill. Brenda noticed that her behaviour was different to mine at various events. Then, she confessed that she dreaded walking into a room of complete strangers. She was convinced that she never appeared at her best when meeting new people. In short, whatever she did, she felt that opening up was an unhappy choice between either clamming up or making a fool of herself (with a varying amount of alcohol involved in either case). So, we began to contrast our differing attitudes.

First, she was incredulous that I could enjoy any event at which I knew, in advance, I would not know a soul. When I told her that, for me, this made the event even more enjoyable because of the exposure to a whole new selection of people, she was even more amazed. 'But when I do that,' she said, 'all I can think of is how terrified I'll be.' Then she paused for a moment and said, 'Basically, I just don't believe I'm interesting enough to carry it off, so everyone will laugh.'

Now, I had always felt this person to be one of the liveliest people I knew. She has a keen sense of humour and razor sharp insight and she is not exactly the kind of lady that is likely to make her companions fall asleep. I challenged her on this and waited for several seconds for her astonishment to subside. 'But that's not how I feel,' she continued, 'I was really shy as a child and my mother always used to tell me off for being reserved with strangers and not speaking up for myself. Ever since then I suppose I've thought that I'm useless at big gatherings.'

Why mention this story here? It provides a very good example of the way in which a negative attitude or belief can affect our behaviour, leading us to restrict ourselves unnecessarily as various opportunities arise in life. It so happened that Brenda's belief had been formed some years previously but this need not necessarily be the case. If you were wondering, learning to socialise successfully will not require you to delve deeply into past memories. Discovering the attitudes that currently drive your behaviour will be enough to enable you to make swift and easy changes.

What are 'beliefs' and 'attitudes'?

The question 'What is a belief?' could in itself take several books to answer, as well as being more suited to a philosophy tome than a practical guide. In this context, I'm using 'beliefs' and 'attitudes' interchangeably to refer to the 'glue' that holds a person's thoughts in a particular shape. These, in turn, may well lead them to behave in a particular way, whether they are aware of it or not. For instance, part of the reason that early mariners did not attempt to cross great oceans was based on their belief that the world was flat, therefore, if they sailed too far, they were likely to fall off the edge of the earth. Strange though those beliefs may seem to us today, they held sailors firmly in place. It was only when the post-Renaissance explorers were prepared, quite literally, to expand their horizons and work with the possibility of a spherical earth that the great voyages began. For the would-be party animal, this demonstrates the power of a belief system.

Here's how it can go

Sometimes, the effect of a belief is wholly positive. For example, someone who believes 'I am always popular and people enjoy talking to me' is likely to smile and engage with people at parties and other social events. This may even mean that an important person at a function approaches them. By important here, I mean important to them, for whatever reason. I know someone who was smiling as she walked into a room because she had been having a great day. The result was that the person who noticed her became her future husband.

Even if this open and friendly attitude doesn't lead to love at first sight or even contract at first sight if you're networking, then you'll certainly speak to the people you need to more quickly than your more fearful brethren. In turn, such a conversation may well open the door to a whole new opportunity that came about as a consequence of the belief in their popularity.

Not surprisingly, this means that people holding positive beliefs about social events are also more likely to enjoy themselves as they're partying, although they will probably never have needed to analyse why this is so. Their positive beliefs then feed back into their attitude to the next occasion and the benefits gather momentum.

The less-than-pleasant alternative

By contrast, someone who thinks 'I will make a fool of myself at this event' is actually more likely to turn the statement into a self-fulfilling prophecy. If you run these words through your mind, you'll notice that your body tightens and the tightening is accompanied by a great rush of unpleasant 'fight or flight' chemicals into the bloodstream. If enough of this tension accumulates, the person with the belief will become much more nervous, perhaps even fearful. This will probably lead them to appear withdrawn, so that others feel less inclined to approach them. Then the situation could well spiral downwards, with that person holding the belief that 'I must be making a fool of myself, or people would be talking to me'. They may then become even more nervous and succeed in providing evidence to support their belief as, for example, when a person's understandable nerves cause them to spill a glass of wine over the very person whom they badly wanted to impress. Consequently, this will make them even less sure of themselves next time, thereby increasing the evidence for and the strength of their negative belief.

Why all this matters

So, the most important point about beliefs and attitudes for the purposes of this book is not so much the nature of them or the reasons why they occur, as the behaviour that they produce. As we've just seen, positive beliefs mushroom into positive circumstances, while negative beliefs spiral downwards into the classic 'vicious circle'.

It would be understandable at this point, if you were a little mystified. Why on earth would anyone want to perform in a way that was not serving them as well as it could? The answer here is simple: beliefs are often, perhaps even usually, not based on any objective evidence whatsoever. In this instance, the person's behaviour at the start of this chapter (i.e. avoiding large gatherings of strangers) flew in the face of the evidence of an impartial bystander's opinion that she was, in fact, lively, witty and interesting. Often, the lack of rationality behind a belief, as demonstrated above, serves only to increase its power, whether the belief is positive or negative.

Beliefs are powerful and positive beliefs about parties, people and the juxtaposition of the two are likely to serve you better than negative ones. So, how do you go about changing existing beliefs into ones that will serve you better?

When they first hear about the concept of belief change, some people are a little wary. They say that it sounds just too close to brainwashing for comfort. In any event, as we've noticed, the beliefs you hold give you a reassuring sense of the shape of the world. In addition, people often seem afraid that changing their beliefs would be a) difficult and b) uncomfortable but, as the song goes, 'it ain't necessarily so'. At the end of this chapter, you're going to be able to begin to change your beliefs consciously, in three easy stages. However, unconsciously, you are already an expert in belief change.

The fact is you have been changing your beliefs throughout your entire life, while remaining blissfully unaware of the process. For example, I can remember, as a five-year-old, being in awe of my teacher's nine-year-old daughter. Her self-assurance and superior clarinet playing skills were quite enough to convince me of two things. First, I was sure that nine-year-olds were incredibly sophisticated, almost godlike, in their wisdom. Second, I was certain that all I needed to do was blow out nine candles on a cake in order to play like a budding virtuoso. Not surprisingly, I had to revise both these beliefs before the age of ten but, in no way did I do so consciously.

The point of this story is simple. Every single time you eat at a new restaurant, alter your hairstyle or choose a new holiday destination, a belief-change process is at work. There you are, holding your particular opinion and you always go to France for your holiday, believing that it is the best option for all concerned and cheaper than Italy. Then, your partner suggests that Italy would, in fact be better value this year. You become open to the idea of a new possibility, first, on cost grounds and, also, perhaps, because your partner would like to try a new destination. As the idea grows on you, you find yourself wanting to believe in the new possibility and, mysteriously, you start gathering evidence to support it. Maybe you suddenly see a special offer in a travel agent's window or find yourself listening to a relevant TV programme more intently.

As the next stage of the cycle begins, the evidence supporting your belief mounts up and you find yourself agreeing that Italy would be a good choice. At the point when you book the holiday, the good value of France becomes something that you merely used to believe, with the cost-effectiveness of Italy (for this year at least) being firmly established in your mind. It then may, in its turn, be superseded by another destination, which it probably will be, because constant change is one of the only things in the universe of which we can be absolutely sure. Without these changes, I might still believe that nine-year-olds can rule the world and you might only ever have one holiday destination.

'Ah,' I hear you cry, 'this might work fine for mundane change but the party thing, or getting on with complete strangers … that's different. It terrifies/bores/exhausts me.'

Trust me, whatever the belief being changed, the process is exactly the same. In fact, by buying this book, you have already set the cycle of change in motion. You must already be open to the belief that learning to socialise for success is possible. If this were not the case, you would not have bothered to invest in this book in the first place.

So, as you are already well on your way, what further steps do you need to follow in order to give yourself the different kinds of belief that will support your socialising? First, you will need to step back and note your existing beliefs. For instance, if you currently believe that you are dull at parties, (or any other event, for that matter), this would equate, in our example above, to the person who believed that France was always the cheapest option. However, you need to identify that belief before you can work with it.

The next activity is designed to help you do just that. Again, it is purely for your own benefit, so please be as honest with yourself as you can. You might also like to try sticking with the first answer that springs to mind. When you're dealing with beliefs, it's usually the most accurate.

What are your beliefs about the idea of being the 'life and soul of the party'?

Take a blank sheet of A4 paper. On it, complete each of the following sentences in a way that best describes your beliefs. Use any words that best express your opinion.

1. If I were to become the life and soul of the party,

a) the best thing about it would be ...

_____

b) I'm not sure that I'd like ...

_____

c) I feel that I would have to ...

_____

d) I believe that others would ...

_____

2. Other beliefs I have about social situations are:

_____
_____
_____

Notice how your beliefs already seem easier to tackle now that they are written down.

Now that you know the basic framework, you are ready to go further. You are already, by definition, open to the idea that your beliefs about yourself, social events and being the life and soul of the party can change. In a sense, much of the rest of this book is dedicated to providing you with the confidence, techniques and evidence to enable you to convince yourself that you can socialise successfully. It is only when you actually *get out there* that previous concerns about socialising can be laid to rest as something that you used to believe. However, you can prepare the ground in a way that will make the changes even more swift and easy by carrying out the next two activities as well.

What would you like to believe?

Your next task is to decide which positive beliefs you would like in the place of the negative ones. At this stage, do not worry about whether or not they appear to be rational and reasonable. Just concentrate on deciding which beliefs you'd like to have.

While you are choosing them, bear in mind that your beliefs, like your aims from the last chapter, should be wholly positive in nature. For example, it is more effective to believe that 'people like me', rather than think 'people aren't laughing at me' because, in this second thought, the use of a negative, even in a positive way, weakens the effect of the belief.

Here are examples of the kind of positive beliefs and attitudes that you might want to grab instead. You may choose these ideas if you wish or use your own but, above all, choose beliefs with which you feel comfortable.

Examples

'I can get on with anyone.'

'I always have a good time at parties and social events. I always meet pleasant, interesting people, including people who often help me achieve my goals.'

'When I'm at an event with other people, I am relaxed, friendly and approachable.'

'When I socialise, I listen and chat easily.'

'People fascinate me.'

'I really enjoy parties.'

When you have chosen your new beliefs, write them out on a separate piece of A4 paper.

Beginning your belief change

1. Choose a quiet time and room or outside space where you will not be disturbed.
2. Take with you either a box of matches/cigarette lighter or a bowl of water.
3. Take out your lists of positive and negative beliefs.
4. In one corner of the room place either a fireproof container or the bowl of water.
5. Place your list of positive beliefs as far as you can from the container or bowl.
6. Pick up your list of negative beliefs. Standing over the container or bowl, read through your list. Notice any feelings, images or sounds that come to mind as you do so.

7. Make a conscious decision that you are ready to get rid of these old beliefs and memories.

8. Destroy the piece of paper carrying the negative beliefs in the way that feels most effective to you. If you feel comfortable with this, set light to the piece of paper within the fireproof container. If fire makes you nervous, you could instead watch your piece of paper dissolve and turn into mush in the bowl of water.

9. When the paper has been destroyed, notice how light you feel and the space inside yourself that is ready for the new positive beliefs.

10. Turn your back on the bad beliefs and walk slowly and purposefully towards your new ones.

11. Pick up the piece of paper with your positive beliefs and read them out loud. Feel the new beliefs beginning to become a part of you as you do so.

12. If any positive images, sounds or feelings come to mind as you read the list, remember and record them, perhaps on the piece of paper in your hand.

13. The first part of this activity is now complete. However, you can strengthen your new beliefs more quickly by reading them out loud (again, in a place where you will not be disturbed) twice a day, ideally, on waking and before going to sleep. Only stop this process when you feel that your status as the life and soul of any party you choose is so obvious that you do not even need to think about it.

If these exercises have completely changed your beliefs, congratulations. If not, stay calm. They are designed primarily to help you begin to alter your position and will be built upon and used again in the following chapters. That process begins with a way to make socialising so enticing that, from now on, you'll volunteer to do it.

Chapter Two

Create Your Carrot

So, now you know what you want and you've got nothing, or at least much less in the way of mental baggage blocking your way, you're raring to go to that next party ... or perhaps not quite yet. The fact is that you may already be feeling much better (and it's possible that you *did* just shout, 'Yes, take me to that party – I'm ready', in which case, I'll see you there). However, it is more likely that you're feeling open to the idea but not quite as comfortable as you want and deserve to be about the whole concept. That is fine because, although you've made a great start by getting this far, there's more to come.

First, it's time to make the idea of being the life and soul of the party really attractive for you personally. The question is, 'How?' As motivational gurus are always telling us, people motivate themselves either with a reward or 'carrot', or an internal threat or 'stick'. Now, I'm not sure about you, but my feeling has always been that parties and 'threats' or 'sticks' just don't mix. So, it's now time for you to create a nice, juicy carrot that makes you salivate at the prospect of going out to that next party or event.

Why create a carrot?

'Hang on a minute,' you may be thinking, 'didn't we just set out where we wanted to go?'

Yes, you did decide to go there but this chapter's all about how to enjoy the ride.

Think about this. A few years ago, I introduced these ideas to someone who had sought me out simply by saying, 'I'm not very good at this kind of thing … I know I'm not and I need to be.'

I couldn't refuse him help, although, looking at him, I had to wonder if my enthusiasm meant we might both end up biting off more than we could chew. This absolutely wonderful man physically shook when he spoke to strangers and consequently, only ever took on the 'back office' roles where he worked, even though he was one of the brightest and most experienced people there.

We got going but, although he seemed very willing to follow my suggestions, his heart just didn't seem to be in the process at all. Finally, I sat him down and asked him why he'd *really* got in touch with me.

'Well,' he said, 'this company's been going through some tough times and I was afraid that if I couldn't do more sales work, I'd lose my job.' Then everything fell into place. He had a powerful enough reason to start the process but his main motivation was clearly going to be fear rather than pleasure: not a great starting point if he wanted to be the 'life and soul' of most places, least of all a party.

'Listen,' I said, 'I think you're fantastic and these people clearly need you whether you can charm the birds from the trees or not. I'm sure you can also learn how to show other people how fantastic you are but only if you really want to and have a real reason for doing it that excites you, rather than just to avoid more problems.'

After much thought, he decided that it would also mean a lot to him to become a real part of his local community. He could easily visualise the difference it might make to his family where his heart and enthusiasm *really* lay. From that moment on he became one of the fastest learners of this system that I've ever been privileged to teach and he did join in with more community activities. Just for the record, far from being made redundant, he was promoted.

The point of this story, if you haven't already guessed, is that carrots really work. In fact, they work in lots of situations but none more so than parties and people's social lives. They're of the perfect scenario to practise the 'no pain, no gain' technique, because enjoyment, the whole point of a party, shows up in your face, speech, actions ... everything that sums you up at that moment.

So, if you're the kind of person for whom 'no pain, no gain' is a bit of a mantra, you might also want to review this as we move forward. Pain and parties simply don't mix. You won't suddenly get the partner of your dreams, an amazing contract or simply the most interesting friend you've ever met, by dutifully forcing yourself to x number of events a year and keeping a fixed grin on your face worthy of a politician, while all the time wishing you were back at home.

It simply doesn't work that way. Enjoyment is heartfelt ... that's why we're talking about life and soul here.

Create your carrot ... easily

Luckily, it is incredibly easy to begin to enjoy social events in a genuine way that's appropriate for you, even if you never have. In fact, the method is so simple that it requires no financial outlay, no back-breaking labour and no drastic change of personality. All you will need are a few minutes of concentrated thought in order to carry out the activity at the end of this chapter.

The method is easy to demonstrate. Think for a moment about an activity you enjoy. This could be anything from gardening to driving, rambling, or just about anything else you care to consider. I know one person who, when asked a similar question, thought of the great satisfaction they gained from doing the plumbing in their home. The actual subject doesn't matter. What counts is how it makes you feel. If the activity you have in mind leaves you feeling enthusiastic and full of the joy of living, then concentrate on it for a moment.

It is highly likely that the way you view your enjoyable activity differs a great deal from your perception of social events but, if you can superimpose the positive feelings of your preferred activities, things will change. Now, if you picture the event, it is probably brighter, sharper and clearer than the previous representation. You may even become a part of the scene in your mind, rather than just an onlooker. The other people in your mind's eye will be of normal proportions and size and their speech or any other background features will be harmonious and broadly positive. You will probably begin to feel enthusiastic, smiling inwardly and outwardly in your new relaxed state.

Although it may be rather unfair to drag you away from this pleasant experience, the point of the exercise has probably become clear. The way in which we represent concepts to ourselves makes an enormous difference to our feelings about them. As you saw in the last chapter, feelings, whether internal or external, influence our performance. Therefore, creating a feeling to support your new beliefs about socialising will boost your confidence and your success.

Why does this work?

In case this all seems rather too good to be true, consider the scientific evidence for the efficacy of this and similar forms of 'mental rehearsal'. In his book *Mind Sculpture*, Professor Ian Robertson (1999) cites the case of a javelin thrower who, because of an injury, was unable to train in the crucial weeks prior to a major competition. Having little to do with his time during his enforced rest, he began pretending that he was actually competing. Step by step, he went through each stage of his event at the same speed as if he were actually doing it. This thought process seemed to work to the point that his sprained ankle no longer affected his image of his performance. At the championships, he achieved a placing unheard of for someone who had done so little training. He attributed his success to having trained for the competition in his mind. Professor Robertson then goes on to explain how mental rehearsal causes brain cells to become used to working together in new ways so that, once it is time for the actual performance, very little extra effort is needed.

Make it compelling

What then, is the relevance of all this to parties and social events (unless of course, you always carry a javelin with you when you go to them ... just in case)?

Seriously though, the javelin story has some clear parallels here. First, mental rehearsal provides an easy way for nervous partygoers to gain confidence and actually increase their chances of having a good time. Second, a compelling concept puts you into a much more resourceful state of mind. Did you notice how much more positive you felt when you were thinking about your preferred activity just now? The importance of this is not just that your family, friends and colleagues will find you easier to live with as a social event approaches (a useful by-product of the process), nor is it the bonus that compelling representations are just so pleasant to consider that you want to keep re-visiting them. By creating a concept of being the life and soul of the party that feels, looks and sounds compelling, you are effectively creating a magnet that draws you towards turning it into reality. This is because, as explained in the last chapter, negative feelings and beliefs turn into vicious circles, whereas positive feelings and beliefs multiply. By creating a concept of socialising that you personally find attractive, you are giving yourself an opportunity to break any vicious circles and start boosting your confidence.

Third, if you allow yourself to keep viewing socialising in a negative way, you run the risk of creating another cycle in the vicious circle. Think back to the last chapter. Remember the person who was so anxious not to make a fool of themselves that they ended up spilling wine? Well, in addition to their beliefs, the odds are that they were running a pretty unattractive mental scenario prior to that event, in order to fulfil their own prophecy so efficiently.

Common concerns

Often, at this stage of the process, would-be partygoers shake their heads. They ask themselves why they aren't as enthusiastic as they thought they should be? The important thing to remember here is that everyone is different. This means that everyone views events in a different way. Therefore, take your cue from whichever of your senses dominates your memory of a compelling activity and pay attention to that one. You don't have to focus on a picture in your mind's eye. You might recall background music more vividly, the warmth of a room or even the taste of the food. The point about a memory that works is that the result must make the event something that draws you closer to it. So concentrate on whichever part of an experience does that for you.

Alternatively, you may well be saying something else, perhaps along the lines of, 'It's all very well for you to talk about making these pictures and dreaming about them. I wish I could get that far. Every time I try, I just get a re-run of last year's Christmas party, when I asked the boss how his mother was enjoying herself. She turned out to be his wife.'

In addressing a concern like this, I would first of all congratulate this person. They have already mastered the art of creating a representation of an event and are well versed in running it again and again. Now all they need to do is turn this skill around so that it boosts their confidence, rather than undermining it. However, this will be small comfort to someone who was clearly very embarrassed at the time and may still remain so.

The value of embarrassment

The golden rule to remember in circumstances like this is that even embarrassment has a positive function. Strange as it may seem, the brain does not retain information for the sole purpose of allowing you to beat yourself over the head with it. That would go against the broad human instinct for self-preservation. Instead, in the context of having fun, it is almost certain that you will have retained the memory because there is something that, consciously or unconsciously, you need to learn from it so that you can go on to have more fun, more easily, in the future. Once you are conscious of this learning, you'll find you are able to let the memory go much more easily, rather than indulge in unpleasant re-runs of the event.

As memories are extremely personal and subjective, it is not the place of any other individual to predict the education they might offer to the person who holds them. The same event could be subject to a variety of different interpretations. For example, the person interacting with their boss might, in retrospect, have learnt a number of things from that event. They may conclude that it is better to ask directly how that individual is feeling, in which case they may have discovered that they were referring to someone's wife.

A couple of other interesting aspects present themselves in relation to this 'boss's mother' event from which any partygoer can take a lot of encouragement. First of all, while it is useful to be as perceptive as possible at social events (easy routes to which will be explained later) mind-reading is not a required skill and is best avoided. In one sense, our poor partygoer was mind-reading from the first. We don't know that the boss was perturbed by the remark. While I suspect that many, if not most people would fear the worst after making such a comment, it is possible that the boss himself was not bothered. Maybe other people had made the same mistake, maybe he secretly agreed that his wife looked old, or perhaps there was a considerable age gap between the couple (and why not, by the way?).

By automatically attaching dire consequences to a comment, a partygoer is imposing their opinions on someone else who may think quite differently. Therefore, they may well be suffering more as a consequence of the comment than the person to whom it was made. This brings me on to the most likely outcome of all.

Memories can be shorter than you think

In all probability, the remark may well have offended the boss, briefly. He may have held it in his mind for, at worst, a few weeks but, although the comment may play a central role in the mind of the person who made it, other concerns are more likely to supersede it in the boss's mind. Mortgages, meetings, crises and joys would probably have replaced it. However, the comment has assumed such central importance in the mind of our embarrassed questioner that it is clouding his view of other social interactions. These would, if he but knew it, have the potential to bring fresh opportunities for enjoyment and success, rather than paralysing him in terror.

So, once you feel you've learned all you can from an unpleasant memory, let it go and replace it with something better. It has had power over you for long enough. Everyone makes mistakes but the easiest course of action is to learn from them and move on.

Potential emotional baggage around social events falls into two main categories: feelings and attempts to mind-read. Let's take them in that order.

Potential item of baggage one: feelings that limit you

If letting go isn't your strongest point, remember that you share this with a huge section of the human race. You're likely to be hanging onto these memories for all the best reasons ... to avoid a repeat performance, to spare others from real or imagined hurt and a myriad of others.

The problem is that the energetic charge that you're getting from hanging on to this feeling is actually affecting no one but you. Here's one way to discharge it but keep an open mind as you read it. Just try it out because, for the vast majority, it works really well.

Emotional baggage clearance

1. Think of and experience a feeling or emotion that you'd like to change or get rid of completely.
2. Ask yourself, if that feeling were a 'thing' in the space in front of you, what would it be?

3. Be aware of how you think it would look, sound, taste, smell and feel, how light or heavy it might be and whether you'd want to touch it or not.

4. Pretend that you can talk to this 'thing' and ask it what its positive intention has been in hanging around for so long.

5. Let it reply ... it might do so in words or in some other way, such as bringing a particular memory to mind, or changing shape.

6. Thank it. Then begin thinking about a way in which the 'thing' might be appealing to you (e.g. if it changed shape, smelt pleasant, was good to touch etc.).

7. It may begin to change its form all by itself. If not, negotiate some more with this 'thing'. Remember that this is your mind and you can bring in any other *imaginary* tools and resources to help you. For example, you might need to heat up something with a fire, tear something down with a bulldozer or clip something with a pair of shears.

8. Persist with this exercise in a playful way until you feel really comfortable and the 'thing' has either transformed or removed itself to your satisfaction.

    People often ask whether they should get rid of the 'thing', put the transformed 'thing' back into a part of their body with their imagination or carry it round in a different form. The truth is that I can't answer this for you, because the 'thing' with its variants and properties belongs to you, not me. But I can be confident that, if you follow your instincts, you'll do what is best for you.

9. The choices are all yours but this activity is complete when you feel comfortable enough to return to your everyday life and confident that the original feeling has either disappeared completely, or changed radically.

Potential item of baggage two: mind-reading

I often find that the slips from which I learn most are those where I've made a misguided attempt to guess what someone else is thinking. I once went to a party where two other guests were a friend and her new boyfriend. Above all, I was anxious to make her new boyfriend feel welcome. Unfortunately, I launched in with the almost unconscious assumption that he would feel better if he knew we'd already heard about him, as this would have been my reaction. 'Hello,' I said brightly. 'It's great to meet you. I've heard so many good things about you,' which was quite true. It turned out that he was very nervous and the idea that everyone knew about him made him even more so. Fortunately, it ironed itself out and I was able to remind myself that listening first, rather than steaming ahead, will always make the right approach obvious.

There's much, much more on listening in Chapter Three but for now the golden rule is: listen, in order to *check* how someone else *really* feels. Their reaction is unlikely to be a carbon copy of yours and may even be wildly different.

Finding advantages

Occasionally, you may even be able to turn a mistake to considerable advantage, whether it originates from incorrect mind-reading or some other error. I am a notoriously clumsy drinker. If Alice's little bottles said 'drink me', then my wine glasses certainly carry a 'spill me' tag. I justify this by telling myself that I'm so engaged in the conversation that I don't notice when my gestures are about to send something flying. Anyway, it is clumsy. One evening, I pulled off this trick, right down the suit of the man to whom I was speaking at the time. Genuinely horrified, I apologised and offered to get his suit dry-cleaned. He accepted. This of course, meant that I got to know his address and contact number. In fact he remains in my email address book to this day.

Of course, my advice here isn't that spilling wine glasses is the hitherto overlooked key to being the life and soul of the party. Quite the reverse but, given that mistakes will always happen, if you can see any way to turn a situation to your advantage, however potentially embarrassing, then go for it. As long as no one else loses out, seize the opportunity to turn things around.

My mother brought me up to believe that every disadvantage contains within it the seeds of potential advantage. Occasionally, this belief led me to strange habits, such as thinking that all night essay writing at college gave me a great opportunity to watch the dawn for which I was never usually awake. However, in the context of social events, it holds good and is a useful tool in forming a compelling representation of partygoing in all its forms. After all, if you wanted a relationship with someone else whom you found attractive, you probably wouldn't start the conversation by saying, 'Well, before we get into this, I must tell you that I bite my nails constantly and have a real temper.' You would start with your good points. Then, if you had to make reference to anything else, you would still be likely to present it positively. So, in this example, nail-biting would just translate into being a sign that you have lots of excess energy and the temper would simply render you 'passionate'.

In the same way, when you are forming your compelling representation of yourself as a social animal, focus on good points first. For example, think about how people often compliment you on, say, your voice. Then, if you must think about a so-called disadvantage, then turn it into an advantage first. Maybe you are very tall and embarrassed about your height. First of all, it is likely that you are much more aware of this than other people are (rather like the person who took the 'boss's mother' event to heart). Even if this isn't the case, consider how you might think about this more positively. Could other people think of you as 'statuesque'? Could it be useful to have other people looking up to you as you socialise for success? Get into the habit of *really* seeing yourself as others see you, rather than mind-reading with little evidence. I guarantee that your confidence will soar.

With these concerns cleared, you're now ready to begin to build a compelling representation of being 'the life and soul of the party' in your mind.

Create that carrot

1. Find a quiet place where you are going to be undisturbed for at least 20 minutes.

2. Close your eyes and relax by taking some slow deep breaths.

3. Then, visualise yourself doing an activity that you really enjoy. Really imagine yourself carrying it out and be in the experience, rather than just an onlooker.

4. As you think about that experience, notice what you are seeing. Are there colours and, if so, how bright are they? Is there any sound and, if so, in what way is it making this memory more pleasant for you? How do you feel, both in terms of sensations in your body and emotionally? Are there any associated smells and tastes? Be aware of every piece of sensory information that is giving you this positive memory.

5. When you are as fully aware as you can be of your experience, begin to smile and, as you do so, imagine that every positive aspect of this experience is being locked into your smile. If you were already smiling (as is likely) then keep smiling and continue to lock in the experience.

6. Then open your eyes, return yourself to normal and change the focus of your attention for a few minutes. You may wish to walk around the room, jump up and down, or stare out of the window.

7. Then, repeat stages one and two of this process until you are thoroughly relaxed.

8. Next, allow yourself to consider your perfect party or social event. See yourself, happy, smiling and surrounded by interesting people. Add in as much colour as will make the event seem inviting for you. Hear yourself speaking to other people easily and naturally and their appreciative voices as they talk to you. As you do this, begin to smile, if you have not already done so, safe in the knowledge that this smile will bring with it all the positive feelings from other aspects of your life. Mix those feelings into your daydream and add in any others. How warm is the place in which the event is happening? Are you shaking hands with anyone? Is there any other movement, such as dancing? Remember also to add in smells, perhaps of perfumes or flowers, and the taste of any food or drink.

9. Make sure that you are in this experience and not just an onlooker. When you think it is at its peak, fix it into your smile also.

10. When you are ready, slowly come back into the moment and open your eyes.

11. Repeat this exercise at least once a day until you feel automatically, genuinely, like the life and soul of your perfect party, every time you smile.

Chapter Three

Everything But the Words

'Great!' you may be thinking. 'We're on to the practical bit ... my event's tonight and I really need this ... *now*.'

Trust me, the stuff we've been doing was worth it, just like laying foundations for a building. It may not be so exciting or so easy to see the progress but it underpins everything.

So, as I tell you that this chapter is about communication strategies – but the largely silent ones – you may have mixed feelings, frustration even. However, if you look at it in one way, you picked up this book because of the block between you and being your true self at parties. So, frustration and a desire to get cracking with the real party stuff is solid progress. Added to which, if you remember, a couple of chapters back we talked about people dancing on the table and being ultra-extrovert who were not necessarily being the 'life' and definitely not the 'soul' of any party? Read on and you'll experience just how easily, subtly and with bags of integrity you can blend in with, move and become an influential part of any event ... without saying a word.

There are some key ideas that make this possible, so let's move straight into exploring them.

Idea one: rapport without words

The single most frequent comment that I hear from people who are nervous about socialising is that they dislike talking and, therefore, perceive themselves to be at a social disadvantage. If this seems familiar, take heart. Only a small percentage of the initial impression we make on others involves any substantial degree of verbal input. The rest, if we are to believe the statisticians, relies on body language, which is responsible, apparently, for at least 60 per cent of all our first impressions. Building rapport is a classic example of such a strategy and a cornerstone of many other skills.

While it sounds sophisticated, rapport is no more than paying another person or group of people the compliment of meeting them where they are, physically and mentally, at a given time. The reason why this is so powerful is that people tend to like others who they perceive to be similar to them. If they did not, they might have to decide that they themselves were unpleasant, which would be unlikely.

How do you begin to establish physical rapport? To take a broad example, if another person in the room has a particularly relaxed pose, it would be wise to copy that stance, rather than sitting or standing bolt upright as if you were on the alert. Even if a more upright posture is naturally more comfortable for you, the other person will unconsciously respond to the fact that you have matched him or her by thinking, 'Ah, we move in a similar way. We must be alike ... I like this person, he/she understands me.' What better basis could there be for getting along successfully?

You should also feel reassured that this matching of other's postures occurs quite naturally, as you will see if you observe any group of friends. Their movements turn into a sort of unconscious dance, in which each person's position and gestures reflects those of the other group members. The only difference between this dance and your strategy is going to be your level of conscious awareness of the process.

'Yeah but ...'

Some people feel uncomfortable with this concept. 'Isn't it manipulative?' they ask. My answer is that it will only become manipulative if you choose to make it so. Rapport is a gesture of courtesy and friendship. If you wish to begin believing that people at social events are potential new friends or contacts to whom you wish to be courteous, then knowledge of rapport is part of a helpful, easy and nonverbal path to more pleasure for everyone. As rapport is best learnt by carrying it out, the next activity will help you to practise the process step-by-step.

Getting in step

1. Next time you are talking to a friend or member of your family, become aware of the way they are using their body. You may find the following checklist useful in this exercise:

    - Are they upright, slouched, or somewhere in between the two?

    - What are they doing with their arms and hands? For example, are their arms folded, relaxed or busily gesticulating?

    - If the person is using gestures, what sort of gestures are they?

    - How much energy is the person putting into their conversation and movement? High energy indicators include fast speech, lots of gestures and, sometimes fidgeting. The reverse is true if a person is feeling tired.

    - How much eye contact is the person using?

    - What about the person's legs? Are they crossed or their feet tapping? Or perhaps they are standing and shifting their weight from foot to foot?

2. Next, make a conscious effort to match each element of the checklist in your own behaviour. Please note however, that if you match the other person too slavishly, they are likely to flee: less is more. A good tip is to do something that approximates their behaviour, rather than copying it directly. For instance, if their legs are crossed at the knee, yours might be crossed at the ankle.

3. Be aware of how easily the conversation flows when you establish this kind of physical rapport. Then, deliberately break it for a minute or so. Continue in the same way on a verbal level but mismatch their posture. You'll be amazed at how quickly this affects the conversation and it can also be useful if you are deliberately trying to avoid being sociable.

4. Once you've noticed the effect of step three, revert back to a state of good rapport.

5. Practise establishing rapport with a different person each day in this way. Once you feel confident about doing this during conversations with your friends and family, branch out. Try it out at work, with strangers in a lift or even on public transport. Remember, the technique at its simplest involves no words at all. When you feel really proficient, observe and match ever-smaller details, such as the rate at which a person breathes.

6. Continue with this process until it is automatic at all times, including the social events that would previously have made you nervous.

When you become proficient at putting this idea into practice, you'll wonder how you ever managed without it. Any gathering of people will become much more fun to observe, even if you are not intending to socialise at the same time.

The person on the right, with folded arms and crossed legs, is physically out of rapport with the open, relaxed posture of the person on the left.

The pair are now in rapport. Their postures show that they are comfortable with each other, without the need for one person to copy the other slavishly.

Idea two: positive hovering

Don't let the simplicity of this next idea fool you. It's an absolute favourite with everyone who's done it at seminars. I even know of a couple who got together as a result of one person determinedly carrying it out.

Positive hovering works best for people once they have the confidence to build rapport with individuals. 'This is all very well,' you may then be thinking, 'but what about those little groups that form, the cliques with no name, little huddles of people who all seem to know each other and talk animatedly. I can't just break into them …'

Unhappy hovering: The glum expression and stooping, hesitant posture of this hoverer indicate her uncertainty.

Positive hovering: The upright but relaxed posture of this hoverer shows that she feels in control of whether or not to join the group, and is actively listening to the group's conversation.

Positive hovering is a successful strategy for just this situation. The most important thing is, don't be afraid to 'hover' just outside the group. Contrary to what you may believe, hovering does not make you a social outcast. If you hover purposefully, confidently and with intent, it is the number one way to gather information prior to joining the group. Therefore, when others see you doing it, they won't be looking at an insecure person who feels denied the chance to participate. This is the time to cast aside all those past insecurities about not being with the 'in' crowd at school.

The benefits of hovering

Most importantly, hovering gives you a chance to assess the group before you join it. Who knows, once you have heard their conversation, you may choose to move away. Maybe they are enthusing on the merits of different locomotives, when trains make you feel sick. They have a perfect right to socialise precisely as they choose but so do you. It is true that, by the time you finish reading this book, you will be capable of finding any topic of conversation at least relatively interesting. Otherwise, the hover allows you to remove yourself and hover elsewhere before you end up in the middle of a 30-minute discourse on rolling stock, herb gardens or whatever else is being discussed.

It may be that the practicalities of the situation do not allow you to hear the whole of the group's conversation. Nonetheless, hovering will give you a wealth of information. First, it is likely that you will catch at least some keywords. Second, you'll get a good idea of the prevailing mood of the group. Does the average level of physical energy and expression suggest collective thought, anger, boredom, laughter or enthusiasm?

Third, all the body language indicators that now enable you to have rapport with individuals, apply in a modified form to groups. If the group is mixing well, hovering will enable you to discern a kind of 'group dance' in which all the participants are moving their bodies at a similar speed and in similar, although not identical, postures.

If you need further evidence of this, observe a group of friends in any pub or restaurant. Nine times out of ten they will, for instance, all begin to support their chin on an elbow, or gesture towards their mouth if the person speaking does the same. If you are already practised in noticing these patterns then, if you decide to join a group after hovering, you will be able to blend in your gestures with those of the group and thus gain acceptance, quickly and elegantly.

Positive hovering

Next time you see a group of people talking together, make a decision to hover purposefully and happily. Concentrate on feeling good about hovering although, if it does lead you to be invited into the group, go with the flow. However, the next strategy is designed to give you a powerful, subtle but friendly way in which to join groups easily.

Idea three: join a group with ease

So, assuming that you have decided to join a particular group (and it is your decision), how do you do it? You may not think it helpful to be told that there are as many different ways of doing this successfully as there are people but it is true. My own favourite is to wait until someone says something that, taken out of context, sounds intriguing or, better still, suggestive, such as, '... and then he carried me off'. In fact, the speaker might well have been talking about a paramedic but picking up on it with, 'I couldn't help hearing what you just said ...' will work. It is particularly appropriate if you wish to communicate your sense of humour to the group and have not had chance to follow the conversation in detail.

Above all, choose a way to break into the conversation that works for you. You'll learn more about your unique style in the next chapter. However, if at this stage you'd like suggestions as to some more subtle approaches, try the following, either individually or in combination. They all assume that the people in the group are unknown to you.

Smiling

If in doubt, remember that at the vast majority of social occasions, a smile is a sure-fire passport to social success. If it is sincere, it tells others that you are interested, pleasant and genuine.

Once they know that, they won't be able to resist your advance. Ideally, a smile should be given just after you have made eye contact with a member of the group you are approaching. In addition, of course, you have already locked your beliefs into your smile, so will be accessing resources every time you use it anyway.

'But there's nothing worse than a false smile,' you may be saying. This is true and particularly so now that scientists have discovered that a false smile is actually co-ordinated using a different area of the brain to that which links with genuine emotions (Ramachandran and Blakeslee, 1998). Fortunately, the solution is simple. Feel genuine emotion as you smile. If possible, find something in the conversation around you that interests you, then smile.

If this is not possible (and if it isn't, check with yourself that you're about to join the right conversational group for you), then think about something, anything, that you find genuinely pleasant, enjoyable or uplifting, before you smile. You'll find that this is also a valuable technique if one of your previous issues has been difficulty in looking at others directly.

Information

It may be that, having hovered, you've discovered that you can relate to the conversation and have something to add to it. If so, use the smile to gain entry, listen to others for a while and then make your point. Congratulate yourself for having entered a group seamlessly. Bear in mind, however, that your information should not be forced. Better to gain entry to a group in a different way than to use a piece of information that does not fit into the context and could unwittingly leave you and others feeling disjointed.

Compliments

Compliments, given to a group or, in certain cases, an individual, always go down well if they are heartfelt. The compliment that has been cooked up just to gain entry into a conversation will be detected a mile off. However, if you really do love someone's scarf or agree with a group opinion, go ahead and say so.

The physical approach

Sometimes, the movement and departure of individuals (for example, to find drinks or answer a phone) will give you the chance simply to move from your hovering position to one that is more firmly within the group. You'll then be able to listen to others comfortably and join in as and when you choose.

Food and drink

If a gathering is quite informal, going around with food and drink can be a great way to gain an entrée into a group, particularly if you are the host or hostess. The only point to watch here is that other members may unconsciously assume that you are likely to flit off and do the same for another group and engage with you slightly less in the beginning.

So, now that you have the benefit of these new techniques for entering into a group discussion, it is time to practise them.

Joining a group

1. During the next seven days, find a way of being in at least two situations where you can physically join a group (or ideally, a series of groups). Be creative about finding your gatherings: they exist in

canteens, lifts, queues and congregations just as much as at official social events.

2. Begin, with 'positive hovering' as before.

3. Using the techniques above and any others that occur to you, in each group situation practise hovering until you succeed in gaining what feels to you like a comfortable position as a member of at least one of the groups available to you in that situation.

4. Record how you felt afterwards in the space below or on a separate piece of paper. Find at least five ways your experiences enhance your new positive beliefs about socialising. (Remember to focus only on positive points here.)

_____
_____
_____
_____
_____

Idea four: the art of listening

It was one of the ancient Greek philosophers who first highlighted the fact that Man as a species has two ears but only one mouth. However, then, as now, he remarked that this did not necessarily mean that the mouth was used 50 per cent less. In fact, listening is probably the most crucial component to conversational rapport and the least utilised. It is the area of party-going in which naturally noisy people tend to fall down and, correspondingly, a secret strength for anyone who currently avoids talking.

The logic is simple. Most of the time, anyone who talks needs someone to listen to them. Put this together with the fact that most good talkers do not in fact listen as well as they might and a would-be partygoer has a ready-made role in any conversation. Peta Heskell (2001), the flirting trainer, tells a story of the time when she spent half an hour listening to someone talking solely about themselves. At the end of that time, he turned round to her and told her that she was one of the most interesting people he had ever met. So, if listening is such a golden path to success, what are the nuts-and-bolts techniques that fit together to make the perfect listener?

Be entranced

In the next section, you'll see how to find anyone interesting but, in order to be able to do so, you have to have a good grasp of what they are saying. The easiest way to do that, in the long run, is to concentrate totally upon the other person, their words, emphasis, reactions and information. If you succeed in doing this properly, you could actually carry on listening without being aware of a fire-alarm going off in the background (as actually happened to me on one occasion).

Easier said than done you may think. What if the person is only concerned about chicken-breeding or any other topic in which you may not currently be interested? The trick is, be entranced by the person, rather than the subject. As, in fact, most people will begin to talk about themselves rather than their pet subject after a while, this is easier than it sounds. As a guide, here are a few pointers to help you be genuinely entranced, rather than just appearing to be so.

Concentrate on what people are actually saying. The crucial thing here is to avoid going off into your own little world while the other person is speaking. So, for example, if Bloggs says, 'I really enjoyed visiting Paris last week,' avoid the temptation to start thinking, 'Hmmm. Paris. I remember when I went there ... I wonder if the place that did the great hot chocolate is still there? Can I work it into the conversation?' Instead, just let the information come to you at the other person's speed, without formulating questions, as if the conversation were a road or landscape unfolding in front of you. This enables you to stay with the person, rather than being a few seconds, or even minutes, ahead in your mind. Then, when a question does seem genuinely relevant, you'll automatically make it one that is going to enable the other person to share *their* experience more fully.

General listening techniques

These might include:

- Pretending that you have to give a full report of the conversation to another person afterwards. This will keep you focused on what is being said, rather than upon the possible future direction of the conversation. If you like, you could actually take this a stage further and record as much as you can about a conversation afterwards.
- Asking open questions, such as 'Where?', 'Who?', 'What?', 'How?' and 'Why?' allows the person to expand on the information they have already given.
- Practise responding to the other person just enough to allow the conversation to flow freely. So, nodding and smiling to confirm your understanding becomes far more crucial to the art of listening than any smart replies. If you are the sort of person who feels uncomfortable if they go into a situation without input for any length of time, you might even try experimenting to see just exactly how long a conversation will last comfortably with just minimal but encouraging

input from your side. I guarantee you will be astounded by just how little may actually be needed.

- Listen *beneath* the words to find out what really seems to be important to the person in front of you. Which emotions are they expressing with their words and how? If you're new to this kind of listening, some key pointers are:
    - The pace of a person's speech (for example, many people tend to talk more rapidly when they are excited).
    - The pitch of speech (again, the higher the pitch, in general, the more impassioned the speaker).
    - Pauses, or halting speech.
    - Particular emphasis on given words. Consider, for instance, the world of difference in the meaning if the speaker says,

    '*I* really wanted to do that' (implying that someone else may not have done)

    and

    'I really *wanted* to do that' (emphasising the desire to act in a particular way).

NB. Utilising these techniques effectively gives you the added benefit of much greater communication on the phone too.

- 'Try on' the other person's point of view or stance on a topic. So if, for example, they say, 'I'm afraid of the dark,' ask yourself, 'What else is likely to be true for this person, given that they have said this?' One word of caution here though. It is very easy to stray from this technique, which will leave a person feeling understood, into an attempt to mind-read, which is likely to leave them feeling manipulated. Don't assume too much from a few words and do check back with them to see if you have really understood them.
- Enter into the other person's world as fully as you can. If they are describing something, conjure up as good an impression

of it as you can along with them. Be in their experience with them, rather than a polite outsider. There's an activity coming up that will help you to do just that.

Give back appropriately

When you do respond, use all the skills discussed so far to enhance your communication. If you have successfully gauged the emotional tone of the other person and entered into their world, you may very well find that you are automatically matching that person's body language in a different way. If not, adjust your own.

As we've seen, your positive encouragement and interest may well be all the input that is needed if the speaker is really enthusiastic. However, other ways to give them a boost include:

- Identifying with their experience via one of your own. Women tend to do this more naturally than men and it can be a real bonding experience, as long as you:
  - Make sure that your experience really does relate to theirs;
  - Keep the limelight on them. If they've just had a two-week camping holiday, this might not be the time to talk about your five-star luxury jaunt last year, even if you did both suffer a delayed flight.
- Summarising your understanding of the conversation so far.
- Being who you are. At the end of the day, one genuine reaction is worth a thousand that are phoney or staged. If you've followed the steps given so far, you'll probably have built up enough rapport to disagree on a few points, provided that the disagreement is genuine, polite and not aimed at the speaker personally. It is boredom, rather than disagreement that kills off the majority of conversations

prematurely. The next section will show you just how to ensure that you are never bored at a party again.

Why listening alongside a person is important

Someone once asked me, in all sincerity, why listening in this way was important. As a 'people' person, I was a bit taken aback by the question but actually, it's a great thing to ask. If we don't know why we're doing something, there's always a risk of following an outdated convention or empty rule. And, by the way, just in case you're wondering about the person who asked me, he was a fascinating and witty person, far from anti-social. He was just more focused on concepts and things than people.

So, I thought for quite a few seconds in silence before answering (which, as my husband would no doubt tell you, is a pretty rare thing): 'It honours that person's experience and helps you understand them and the situation better.'

Be aware of your progress

Within the next seven days, hold three conversations with other people. They can be of any length and could be done over the phone provided that, at the end of each of them, you have enough material to fill out the log on the next page:

Date	Speaker	How were they feeling?	How did I know?	I particularly enjoyed …	Other notes

As you interact with people and fill this in, remember to be gentle with yourself. The point is to enhance your skills, rather than to achieve some mythical point of perfection, or give yourself a hard time over any temporary blocks. Just by getting out there with the intention of enjoying yourself, you are making tremendous progress.

The most important column in this chart registers your enjoyment. This enables you to remember that interacting with people, even when you don't have to is now something you enjoy.

If you do think of anything that might have helped you to get on even better, just note it down ready for next time. These experiences are proof that you have already changed and are moving towards new experiences. As such, they are a crucial part of your progress.

Welcome to my world

Over the next day or two, get into conversation with someone else. They could be someone you know well – a colleague, partner, family member – or, if you're feeling adventurous, a stranger. Whoever it is, use your listening skills to get them to talk about something in which they are interested. As they do so, enter their world as completely as you can. You might like in particular to think about:

- The sensory words they use: can you see, hear, feel, touch and taste the things they are talking about?

- The dimensions involved. Often people mark out the ideas about which they are talking in the space in front of them. So, is the current budget quite literally a 'big' problem, or the team's prospects a 'broad horizon'?

- What is the person feeling as they are speaking? (Remember the golden rule: if in doubt, check.)

When you feel you've been able to enter another person's world completely, start making a habit of it in every conversation. It will change your life.

Idea Five: Everything is interesting (yes, really)

So, suppose for a moment that you have made it to a particular function. You walk confidently into the room, observe various groups from a distance, hover around one of them and fall easily into a rapport. Then, the unthinkable happens. Other people melt away and you are left, cornered and trapped, with the infamous party bore. What should you do?

While there are various ways in which you can elegantly extricate yourself from a conversation (and we'll come back to them in a few moments), there is another, often more rewarding option. For now, just allow yourself the flexibility of acting a little differently and behave as if the person in front of you were in fact interesting to you.

You might have noticed a very deliberate choice of phrase there, i.e. 'interesting to you'. For, interest, like time, is a relative thing. You may not be interested in car mechanics or flower arranging but that is the result of your personal thoughts and ideas, rather than the subject in question. The subject itself is essentially neutral and comes to life (or not) via the interaction between both the speaker *and* the listener.

So, what are the steps leading to interest?

1. First, follow the listening strategy carefully (if it doesn't spring to mind easily, this might be a good time to re-read it).
2. Then, be open to the subject and the person in front of you. Effective ways to do this include:
   - emptying your mind of everything but the subject;
   - seeing the subject in bright colours;
   - talking positively to yourself about it;
   - thinking of as many different ways as possible in which the information could be used; and, of course,

- being physically open to the person in front of you, complete with bright eyes and a genuine smile. The exercise below will give you practise in this technique and help you to pick the combination that will work best.
3. If there are points you find boring or don't understand (the two are often intimately linked), don't be afraid to ask questions that will make the subject more accessible. A great question is, 'Why is such-and-such important to you/your organisation etc.?' Once you understand a person's motivation, it becomes much easier to get enthusiastic along with them.
4. In 99 times out of 100, this strategy will leave both parties feeling that they've had a really meaningful exchange.

Benefits

Just in case you're still struggling with this technique, stop to consider a few points:

- As you've already seen, it's possible to establish an unconscious rapport with people by matching their body language. Therefore, if you allow yourself to mirror the other person's interest in their subject in a similar way, they will automatically sustain and increase their level of enthusiasm.
- Even if the information you're getting isn't relevant to you right now, you never know when it might be in the future. The latest cricket or World Series scores may bore you rigid, for example. However, if the next time you have to meet an important potential friend or contact and he or she is a sports fan, this information could be gold dust. (This actually happened to me, by the way, as my father-in-law is an ardent cricket fan. Am I glad that I never dismissed all that stuff about 'overs'.)

- As my Mum used to say when I whinged about being bored during the school holidays, 'If you feel bored, you're boring yourself.' French people might agree with her: *s'ennuyer* in French literally translates as 'to bore yourself' as well as 'to be bored'. Think for a moment about what that means and the empowering potential it gives you to take responsibility for your level of interest in any conversation, whether as a listener or speaker.
- If all else fails, you can always make the conversation a personal challenge. Tell yourself that you *will* find an interesting angle, even if you haven't done so *yet*.
- Much as you may like it to be otherwise, sometimes you can't actually control what another person says. However, this technique does at least extend your ability to control your reaction to the subject in question.

What if a person's favourite subject is themselves?

Let's be realistic here. Many people's favourite subject is themselves (although some will be more honest about this than others). What's more, if you think about it for a moment, this is no bad thing. If we are speaking about ourselves then, to a certain extent, we are exerting our right to be and to enjoy life in the unique way that only we can, just as we would if we were enjoying our favourite meal.

Having said this, we all know that some people can certainly fail to notice when you might want the subject to change from their last hernia operation. This, of course, works both ways and is something to bear in mind when you are speaking. What should you do?

One option is to change the subject, tactfully, by seizing on 'tag-words', will be described later. By doing this, you are quite likely to direct the person towards their passion too. Once there, you are on safer ground as the majority of people find it tough to be boring about their passion.

If this does not achieve best results, as always, there is another option. There is, after all, a positive side to this situation. Usually, we tend to learn more from a conversation if the speaker has some idea of what they are talking about. As they are likely to be the ultimate authority on themselves, you may learn a great deal about the other person during such a conversation, even if they don't communicate the majority of that information through their actual speech. Treat this as a fun and interesting learning experience.

Remember, also, Peta's story and the message behind it: you will always make friends if you let people talk about themselves.

What's more, if you really get interested in the structure of the other person's subject, you pay them the compliment of entering their world. The last activity in this section will enable you to refine your expertise in this area.

Changing the face of boredom

1. Think for a moment about a subject that you would normally consider boring. Instead of dismissing the subject with just that word, catch hold of the way in which you form that thought:

    - How do you feel emotionally and in specific areas of your body? Where is any discomfort located and with what degree of pressure?

    - Does an internal sound (such as a bored voice) accompany the thought? What is the volume, the sound and which direction is it coming from?

    - Do you see any pictures or symbols as part of the thought? If so, what colour, shape, distance and focus do they have?

2. Deliberately distract yourself for a minute or two.

3. Next, repeat the entire exercise in relation to a thought about something that really interests you. It is 99.9999 per cent certain that you will notice dramatic differences in the form of this second thought. Note the key differences in as much detail as you can.

4. Again, deliberately distract yourself for a minute or so.

5. Then, think about your first subject (from step one of this exercise) once more but using the techniques you noted in step three of the exercise. Centre upon how differently you are now experiencing the same piece of information.

6. Finally, imagine yourself talking to someone at a party. They begin to speak about the topic that you used to find boring. Using the mental techniques that you now know can make something sound interesting, imagine yourself being genuinely interested during that conversation.

Different angles

1. Take a few moments to study the picture below.

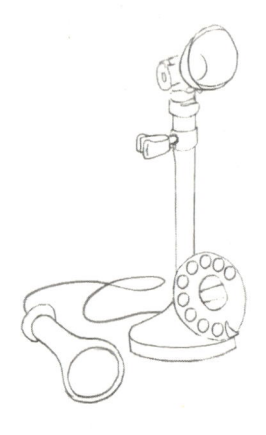

2. Now pretend that you are a journalist or newspaper editor. How many different stories might that picture illustrate?

   _____

3. Note as many as you can but at least seven. You'll be amazed how adept this will make you at finding different angles on the same subject.

   _____
   _____
   _____
   _____
   _____
   _____
   _____

Idea Six: Moving on

Of course, even good conversations have to come to an end. So, even though there's now no need to be bored, you may still need an exit strategy. There is no one way in which this can or should be achieved. However, I always find the following guidelines useful:

- Prior warning. People always seem to respond more positively to your breaking away from an in-depth conversation if you have sown the seeds for your departure earlier, (for example, working into the conversation phrases like, 'I was thinking of leaving at *x time*' or 'I understand *Person Y* is at this event. Have you bumped into him/her yet?'

- *Subtle* distancing via body language, perhaps by moving slightly further away.
- The direct approach: summarising the conversation, stressing how much you've learnt from or enjoyed the conversation and thanking the other person, before declaring your next move.

New conversations

Have a conversation during the next week with someone you would normally have considered boring or, if you like, 'not from my usual circle'. Use as many ideas as you can and notice how differently you think about that person afterwards.

It'll also be great preparation for the next chapter, which is all about how you can use conversation to be the life and soul of an event.

Chapter Four

How to Talk About Anything

So far, much of what we've covered may seem relatively passive. Anyone who started this book may be needing action by now. They may be able to turn up to an event and listen until the cows come home but still need practise in actually saying something. Now it is time for action.

Of course, your confidence in your ability to talk to anyone will have been building up inside you since the beginning of this book, whether you are aware of this or not. These new beliefs and attitudes have been beavering away behind the scenes for a while now, just waiting for this moment.

Conversational tags

The first stage of talking about anything takes us right back to listening. This time, as well as concentrating fully on the meaning of full sentences, you'll also be paying greater attention to individual words, or 'tags'. There are two reasons why this is a crucial part of your toolkit. First, they show where the other person's interests may lie and second, they give you the opportunity to steer the conversation in a direction in which you feel comfortable. Examples of various tags and conversational directions to which they might lead, are illustrated below.

Ending the sentence on a question

Listen for key questions at the end of a comment, such as 'isn't it?', 'can't it?' or 'won't it?'. These are your cues to pick up the conversation by agreeing with the speaker or offering a different point of view.

Emphasis on particular words

Consider the difference between someone saying '*Fred* hated that' (which implies that others may not have done, so opening up an avenue for you to explore) and 'Fred hated *that*', which gives you the opportunity to ask either, why Fred hated that particular thing or, which things it was that Fred preferred.

Of course, if the stressed word is a topic you know something about, it also gives you the opportunity to lead the conversation off again, if you wish. So, if your specialist subject is the nineteenth century and someone says, 'I really enjoyed history ... especially learning about the *nineteenth century*,' then this is an opportunity for you to talk about that period of history as well.

In addition, stress on particular words can often indicate enthusiasm, which will enable you to find the speaker more and more interesting. *What interests each person most?* Have you ever had an experience where a conversation is jogging along quite happily on the lines of, say, house repairs? There you are, debating the merits of plumbers and the other person pipes up with, 'Oh, yes, the guy who came to me had terrible marital troubles.'

Now, although this may seem to you to be a bizarre hijacking of the subject, it is in fact a mine of information. This person is clearly telling you that their focus of interest (either in this conversation, or in life in general) is firmly on the people involved in any incident. Different interests might include:

- **Time** 'Yes, my plumber is always fifteen minutes late ... it was the same last Tuesday.'
- **Place** 'Did you get someone in from that local firm? I used to have someone who only lived at the end of the road.'
- **Cost** 'Does he charge much?'

A few words of warning may be useful here. First, this list of interests, like the conversational tags given above, is not exhaustive.

Second, if a person mentions, for the sake of argument, cost, just once, this may very well be their focus of interest only in this context. Maybe they want to re-do their bathroom and have limited funds. Look for a pattern of interest over the course of a conversation.

Third, even if you think you've detected a pattern, be careful to steer clear of pigeonholing people. Although they often are happiest asking or answering questions on home ground, they may yet want to focus on something completely different.

Have fun with this but take care

Getting in synch with people in this subtle way is exceptionally powerful. So that's fantastic if you genuinely want to have a great time and help others to do so as well. I know of at least one person who got so genuinely interested in other people's points of view by using this technique that they found a new job, a new hobby and a new relationship as a result. All this within a few weeks of one another, after several years of feeling that they 'just rubbed people up the wrong way'.

But focusing on other people's interests can also be a trap: even if the person from the purchasing department is exceptionally attractive, it just might not be you to talk about the cost of things too often ... even if they live, sleep and breathe it. So, be true to yourself and honour the *soul* as well as the *life* section of this process as you put these ideas into practice.

What interests you?

1. Speak about your favourite subject, into a tape recorder for a couple of minutes. Just say whatever comes naturally and disregard pauses or gaps.

2. When you've finished, play back the tape and see if you discover anything about your own focus of interest.

Sizing and levelling

At this stage, you may still be restless. All the exercises above involve tuning in to other people's words. How can this help you to talk about anything?

Focusing on the other person's subjects actually gives you more room for manoeuvre. Here's why (and a friend of mine actually had this conversation).

The people involved were fairly worldly and well travelled and the conversation turned to Papua New Guinea. My friend had to pause momentarily, knowing very little about this part of the world, but she trusted herself. Instead of freezing, blustering or blushing, she simply asked herself, 'What *do* I know about this subject? What associations does it trigger for *me*.' Only one answer came to mind.

She then recounted a story that she had heard about a man fishing there who used dynamite instead of a fishing rod and had her audience rolling around with laughter. In addition, the conversation then turned to the more general topic of environmentally friendly ways of establishing food supplies, about which she did know something.

This episode shows several key ways in which you will be able to talk about anything, provided that you ask those crucial questions (and they bear repeating):

- 'What *do* I know about this subject?'
- 'Which associations does it trigger for *me*?'

These questions work in three separate ways. First, they force you to concentrate on the extent of your knowledge, rather than any lack of it, which, in turn relaxes you, completely counteracting the panic that might have caused you to freeze before you began this book.

Second, they free your mind to approach the subject in a more flexible and playful way. This leads to a more interesting conversation for everyone. For, provided your listeners don't actually need a ball of wool to follow the direction of your thoughts, a new slant on a particular topic may well increase their overall knowledge and set them thinking in new ways. A thought or feeling that is truly your own, simply expressed, will always be original and, therefore, win over your conversational audience, effortlessly and easily.

Finally, because you are staying in control of the topic by selecting it, rather than trying to swim against an uncomfortably strong conversational tide, you are, in fact, less likely to end up feeling ridiculous. This is because you are steering the conversation towards an area in which you feel comfortable (an island in the sea of confusion, if you like). In addition, you are also controlling the level of detail on which you're conversing. Using the Papua New Guinea example, my friend told a general story, whereas a detailed analysis of the genetic basis of crops on the island may have been beyond her experience or knowledge at the time.

Equally, if you do feel more at ease with detail than 'broad brush' concepts, talk about them. Use the ideas in the next strategy to link them to a story that entertains everyone.

Some people might think that widening or narrowing the scope of a conversation could be off-putting, or irrelevant. The real partygoer's reality is very different. By altering the scope of a topic, you're just doing everyone a conversational favour. Conversations have to expand and contract naturally as they proceed. If this did not happen, every subject would become exhausted when the chat had either expanded to encompass the universe, or contracted to the size of individual atoms. What's more, the introduction of a new topic gives a fresh direction to the conversation, before it becomes either cosmic or sub-atomic.

Provided the information you provide is relevant to the subject, you always have the choice of the level at which you respond. Trust yourself and your own choices. If you do, not only will all sorts of information you never realised you could remember emerge from the woodwork of your brain, but you'll also feel happier and more confident.

The exercises at the end of this section will give you all the space you need to practise these techniques even before you encounter another person.

Linkups

This exercise is based on a mind game I used to play as a child. Several of my clients have had a lot of fun practising it by playing this game with their own children. That said, it provides a quick and relaxing tone-up for all kinds of people, anywhere.

1. Think of two separate, completely unrelated, subjects. Picking them from an encyclopaedia, or even the Internet or a business phone directory is ideal.

2. Then, your task is to link the two subjects together in as few steps as possible. The links do not need to be logical in the strict sense, just linked in some way for you. For instance, you might pick 'eggs' and 'sunshine'. I might join these by saying, '(1) Eggs (2) egg-yolk yellow (3) sunshine yellow (4) sunshine.' The only limit here is your own imagination.

3. When this is done in as few steps as possible, either link the same subjects in the same number of steps via different routes, or pick new subjects.

4. Do this for at least three minutes each day until you are absolutely confident that you can always think of something to say, or some link to make on any topic.

Get a word in edgeways

While the majority of tips in this book centre on listening to others and getting them on to their best subject, just occasionally, it can be useful to be able to bring the conversation around to something of your choice. This can be used to ensure that you are speaking from a position of maximum confidence, for instance, or so that you convey an important message. Funnily enough, the ability to steer a conversation seems to be most used when others are talking about themselves.

Steering a conversation is a two-stage process: knowing the direction in which you want the conversation to go and picking up keywords. These are any words that, while they can be associated with the current topic, can also be related to the topic you need to talk about, or with a topic that itself leads in the direction in which you need to steer the conversation.

So, for example, if the hosts at a party are talking about their children and you need to enquire about whether they are still going away on holiday next week (perhaps because you had agreed to look after their place), which options would you have?

You could wait for the conversation to turn to a subject that may be appropriate if you are talking for some time, or you do not need to leave or you could simply change the subject completely, which may work if you really are about to walk out of the door. But the most seamless option would be to steer the conversation, perhaps from the children to school, to school holidays, to holidays, to your role.

This can be represented diagrammatically.

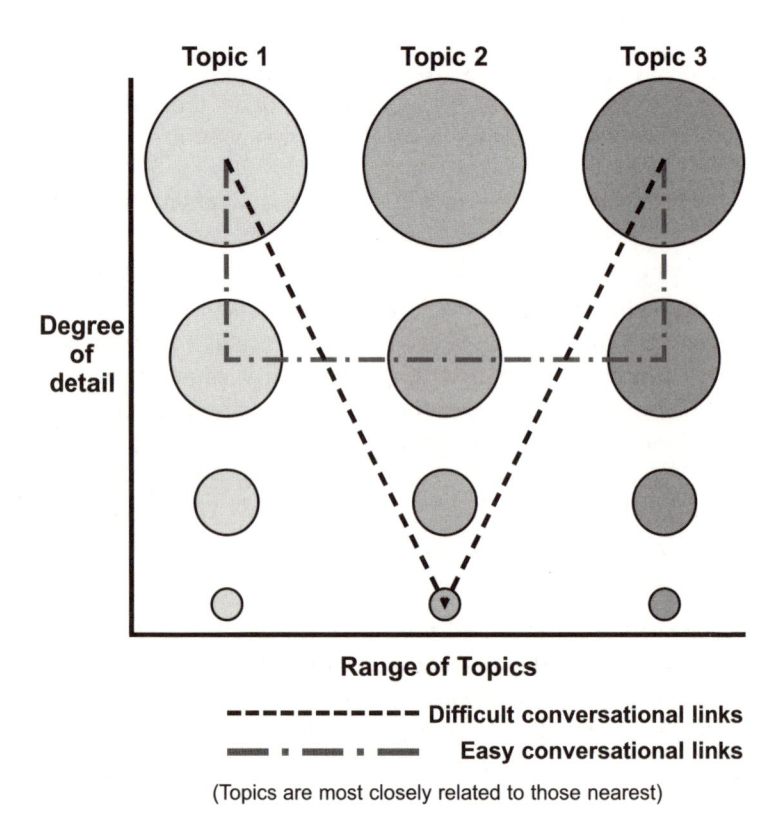

Range of Topics

---------- **Difficult conversational links**
━ ■ ━ ■ ━ **Easy conversational links**

(Topics are most closely related to those nearest)

In order to practise this, repeat the following steps until they come easily:

1. Think of a forthcoming conversation or event where the reactions of people around you will not be crucial.

2. Come up with a list of five completely unrelated words or phrases (using a dictionary or reference book can be useful here). They should also be unrelated to the conversation or event.

3. Your task is now to work into the conversation as many of the five phrases as you can, without anyone else guessing that there is anything unusual about the conversation. This means that you will need to steer the conversation around to topics that will fit the words or phrases in question.

One word of caution: do not overuse this technique, or people will instinctively feel that they are being overruled, rather than heard. Just keep the technique in reserve in case you really need it.

One area in which learning to steer the conversation can be helpful for everyone is that of small talk. Sometimes, it is wholly appropriate for people to chat about how they got to an event, or the weather. So, if people have just arrived or if the tone of the event is light and people are speaking for just a minute or so to several others, it may be apt. I know of one person who, at a very informal barbecue, watched all the newly arrived guests being accosted in turn by an enthusiastic chap, keen to talk about current affairs. Apparently, he hated small talk and was attempting to communicate very genuinely but on a subject that was a little too heavy for people's mood, particularly at the beginning of the evening.

On the other hand, small talk often forces two or more people to get stuck in the same conversational groove from which there appears to be no escape. In this situation, just remember one thing: small talk is usually a cry for conversational help. Therefore, if your groove is fast turning into a rut, let this knowledge inspire you. Be bold and take the initiative by steering the conversation a little. The other person will probably thank you silently and may even follow your lead by bringing up other topics themselves. If you remain sensitive to their reactions at all times, this strategy is a sure-fire winner and improves the event for all concerned.

Finding the right words

For some people, the key issue is to find the right words, any words, at some point before other people in the conversation have hurtled ahead and left you behind.

My husband Jim used to have this difficulty. When he *does* speak he's always really witty and insightful and often able to entertain people with impersonations, including of me. The problem used to be that he took so long thinking about what he was going to say that people were either squirming or moving on to other topics.

One day, I was watching him more closely than usual during one of these pauses. As he was clearly running through the possible comments, his eyes were focused firmly upwards. Yet research on the subject of eye movements (for example, by Robert Dilts) suggests that your brain finds the words most efficiently if you look down to your bottom left in order to hunt for them.

Try it for yourself and be aware of the difference.

Since Jim made the switch to searching for words in a different place, he now makes comments faster and just happens to be more thoughtful than his impulsive and fast-talking wife. As he's also an ex-stammerer, my thought here was that if the idea worked for him, it would work for anyone, which, so far, is proving to be true.

It's often OK to butt in

Talking about Jim also reminds me of the frustrations we had when we first met. I'd be chatting (either directly to him or with him and someone else) and I'd suddenly realise that I'd not heard from him in an obscenely long time. Now, of course, this does show some lack of consideration on my part and I promise I've mended my ways and continue to do so. However, when we explored it, we realised that we had different attitudes to butting in. As a fast talker who enjoys a certain amount of interaction, sparring and verbal excitement, I was expecting Jim simply to butt in when he had an interesting point to make, as I did. As a calm, peaceful and polite soul, he was waiting for a conversational pause that might often simply never come.

The moral of the story is: if you are, as Jane Austen once said of one of her characters, 'a most determined talker' (Austen, [1813] 1992, p. 53), make a conscious effort to leave gaps (and they'll probably seem to you like large gaps) in which other people can have a chance to be the life and soul of the party too. If you're naturally a quieter type, yes, people *do* appreciate your contribution and it's often OK to bring it into the conversation while someone else is drawing breath. After all, if you leave it too long, the conversation will move on and no one will know just how insightful all your careful thinking has made you, which would be a real waste.

Finally, here's the ultimate activity to make you feel able to talk about anything.

Random talking

There is a panel game on the radio called *Just A Minute*, on which each of the contestants is required to speak on a randomly selected subject such as 'Christmas shopping' or 'flowerbeds', for one minute, without 'repetition, hesitation or deviation'. However, in this exercise, you can hesitate, deviate or repeat as much as you like but you do have to:

1. Pick a random subject.

2. Talk about it for at least a minute (either in front of a mirror, or a supportive friend).

3. At first, if a minute is a real challenge, try 20 seconds. Increase this to 30, 40 and so on, until you can reach, or exceed, your one-minute milestone.

Do this activity in relation to two or three subjects at least three times a week, until it is effortless and natural.

Chapter Five

Questions, Questions

Questions are the life blood of great conversations. They can sustain a conversation for hours, help you build on your ability to find other people fascinating and, of course, help you obtain all sorts of information, from the phone number of someone you've fancied for ages to the information that'll help you most at work and everything in between. As they both liven things up and encourage openness, they are a key tool for anyone who wants to put both life and soul into parties. Hence, they get a chapter all to themselves. Actually, as questions can very often be life-changing, such as the 'Shall I emigrate?' or 'Will you marry me?' variety, they probably deserve a whole book. In the meantime, though, here are some thoughts about them from the two main angles: asking and answering.

Your questions

How do you feel about asking questions? If this is already easy for you, you probably need only skim over this section. If, however, they make you feel in the least uncomfortable about them, ask yourself, 'What stops me from feeling good about asking questions?' There are as many answers to this as there are people on the planet, but common initial difficulties with questions include:

- 'I'm sure I should know the answer already.'
- 'I'll look stupid.'
- 'People will laugh at my question.'

Next time you find yourself thinking one of these thoughts, just replace it with any or all of the following ideas. If you do, you may suddenly discover that you've become a person who loves to ask questions.

- The other person may not have expressed themselves clearly. Therefore, in asking for that clarification, I'm increasing the chances that my response will be seen as intelligent.
- I'm probably asking the question(s) that everyone else would ask if they had the nerve.
- If I really know nothing about the subject in question and say so, then my honesty will be refreshing and this will make it even easier for them to feel a rapport with me.
- I really want to know more about this subject. Questions are just such a great way of gaining more knowledge.
- By asking questions, I am communicating to the other person that I am genuinely interested in them and their subject.
- By asking questions, I get more clues about the other person's conversational 'tags', which help me to understand where the conversation might be going.
- If I ask the other person questions, this automatically implies that I am considering them to be expert in some way. This is flattering and pre-disposes them to respond positively.
- I'm naturally curious.

Imaginative questions

Bear in mind, though, that questions are definitely not created equal. One of my clients complained to me recently that they only ever seemed to have dull conversations at his company's social events, before we started exploring ways to liven things up.

'What sort of questions do you ask?' I wanted to know. He paused, then admitted that, 'What project are you working on?' was an industry standard. Apparently, things have warmed up nicely now that questions like, 'What do you dream about doing?' have come into play.

So, especially with people with whom you already know you have some common ground, choose juicier questions. They will yield more interesting answers.

Imaginative questions

1. Give yourself a maximum of two minutes to list the six most interesting questions you could ask of someone else. You could use the 'dream' question as inspiration, or make it more vague, such as, 'What's possible for you?'.

2. The only ground rules are that your questions should:

    a) be open, i.e. force the person to answer with more than 'yes' or 'no';

    b) be different to those you would normally ask;

    c) be interesting but widely applicable, e.g. not just related to your industry.

So, get ready to enjoy asking questions.

Other people's questions

What happens when questions are asked of you? If the other person really is, for instance, thinking of you as an expert, how can you retain your credibility, if you are, in fact, talking about the first thing that came into your head? There are a variety of strategies from which partygoers can choose:

1. Keep trusting yourself and let information flow. If you began by talking about the first story or issue that came into your head, it's likely that you selected it automatically because there is even more knowledge (or related knowledge) where that came from.
2. If you truly don't know an answer, say so. Again, your honesty is a platform on which you can build rapport. It also gives you the freedom to venture an opinion anyway. After all, if you've admitted that you don't know or aren't sure about something, there can be no possible comebacks if you exercise your imagination a little and provide further avenues for your listeners to explore.
3. Another alternative if you are unsure about an answer is to 'play the politician'. Our esteemed leaders are past-masters at getting across the information they want you to hear, rather than answering the question posed. Imitating them too much may lose you friends but they are worth studying in order to pick up three basic techniques:
    (a) *Stalling.* Phrases like 'I'm glad you asked me that' or 'That's an interesting question' give you extra thinking time and are an elegant alternative to 'um'.
    (b) *Rephrasing.* This involves changing the emphasis from the one in the question, to one with which you feel more comfortable. So, for instance, if someone asks, 'What is the prevalent philosophy in business today?' you could say something like, 'That's a very broad question but I can fill you in on the philosophy in our company, which is …'.
    (c) *Turning the question around.* Don't be afraid to say something like 'Why do you ask?' either to seek clarification, or to prevent the other person from being intentionally difficult.

4. This is probably the most important pointer of all. A question almost always contains a useful answer within it. This is a piece of knowledge that trainers utilise instinctively and that, again, will banish blushing and hesitating from your repertoire for ever.

The easiest way to illustrate this point is via specific examples. As with conversational tags, there are three important parts of a question that, taken together, will naturally frame a seamless answer for you:

(a) *The question word.* Does the question contain a clue about the type of answer required? For example, if a person asks 'where' or 'when' something occurred. A 'how' question begs a more detailed description of method. A 'why' question asks for the basis of your beliefs or the logic behind a situation and it may seem the most challenging at first. However, it is, in fact, the question that gives you the most freedom. If an answer is truly uncertain and you apply yourself to answering it as honestly as you can, how can you be wrong?

(b) *The subject.* Treat this part of a question as you would a conversational tag (see Chapter Four) and proceed from there.

(c) *The motivation.* Often, the quickest way to get to the heart of a question is to think about why it was asked. For instance, if you've been talking about making bread, your answer to a question about your oven will vary considerably according to whether the questioner is:

(i) a professional baker;

(ii) an oven manufacturer; or

(iii) a child.

This will enable you to tailor an example just for them, which will make them feel a million dollars and boost your social confidence into the bargain.

Newscasters

1. Listen to a newscaster or presenter as they interview someone. Ideally, you should begin with a radio rather than a TV presenter, as you will not be distracted from the wording of their actual questions. However, in either case, concentrate on the questions they are asking and the responses.

2. As you are listening, fix upon the following points in the questions and the responses:

   - 'The question word'
   - The question content or 'conversational tags'
   - The questioner's motivation
   - The level of detail that the question demands
   - The speed of the answer
   - The level at which the answer is pitched
   - The directness of the link between the answer and the focus of the question.

I guarantee that listening to the very slim links between questions and answers given by those who are experienced in this field, will give you all the conversational confidence you need.

Finally

Remember that questions are supposed to be fun and help you understand more about other people and them about you. This is another plea for you to show your soul if you want to be the life and soul of any party. One genuine question, respectfully asked, is worth a thousand of the 'Do you come here often?' variety. Politicians may be slick with words (and it can be useful to practise some of their word play) but you'll have a lot more fun if you're happy to be yourself, make some mistakes and laugh your way through. By being able to laugh at yourself, you'll also help entertain others, which is the biggest piece of the 'life and soul of the party' puzzle and our next topic.

Chapter Six

A Trip to the Theatre

Despite everything I've said so far about listening, questions and the general fact that 'less is more' at parties and life, what's everyone's favourite image of the 'life and soul of the party'? Every time, it's the raconteur, the storyteller, who is surrounded by hordes of entranced listeners as he or she keeps them entertained for hours on end with the tale of the time when Great-Aunt Bessie lost her teeth behind the sofa.

So, by popular demand, this chapter answers that question of how you become a super-powerful storyteller, with a little help from the world of theatre. But before we go into it, remember one plain and simple fact. You are already a storyteller. If you moaned to your best friend over the phone about the events of your really bad morning, told anyone exactly how you met your partner, or described any incident from your early life, then you've told a story that engaged someone. Therefore, the only question left becomes, 'How can you tell a story in such a way as to keep your audience spell-bound?'

The trick is to break down your storytelling into the smaller techniques that make up the whole.

Theatre and storytelling

Even if you've only been to the theatre once in your life, you'll know that they do things differently there. Normal rules are suspended in order to create an overall effect. By thinking about some of these rules and toning them down to suit a social situation (unless you want to learn lines and so forth), you'll have some great guidelines for telling stories confidently. So, what are the theatrical basics?

First of all, scale. In a theatre, you may be some distance away from your audience. So all gestures and pitch have to be grander and more exaggerated than they might otherwise be. Now, granted, I hope that at a party or event your audience is closer than twenty feet but the principle remains a good one. You're still transferring the contents of your mind into theirs, so a little exaggeration of sight, sound, colour and tone (and only a little) gets the point across nice and clearly and helps you to fit the more conventional picture of the 'life and soul of the party' (if, of course, you want to do so).

Second, there's structure. Plays, musicals and pantomimes have acts, so people know where they are and when they can eat ice cream. In the same way, if your story has structure in the form of a beginning, middle and end, the people listening know where they are in your story and how long it'll be before they can grab one of those interesting nibbles that just went by. If you've ever had the experience of your audience dwindling rather than expanding, chances are that this piece of your strategy was awry at the time. Get this right and people will congratulate you on a tale well told and look forward to the next one.

Structure also means the actors know where the play is going. In the same way, know your story, at least well enough to keep it flowing. Of course, this can be quite a challenge, especially when you really have lost the thread. That's the time to pause, smile and draw upon a nice linking phrase or two that you devised earlier as you wait for inspiration to flow again, as it surely will if you keep calm for long enough. As an experiment, next time you're in a sympathetic group of people, try pausing for as long as you dare and contrast afterwards how long the pause felt to you and your listeners. It's almost certain that listeners will appreciate the chance to process your words.

Remember, they can only feel any of your inner panic if you show it to them, or announce it in some way.

The third theatrical ruse is to grab people's attention and keep it. Just as actors learn to work the audience by looking at different parts of it and holding their attention there for a few seconds, so can you. Just as actors make an entrance, so can you (at least metaphorically) with an attention-grabbing opening line. One person I know started a story by asking, 'Do you know how many germs scientists have found in the average bowl of peanuts on a bar?' and got away with it. (I promise, though, from what I remember, you just don't want to know the answer to that one.)

Just as theatrical props – from a plumed hat to a few abstract white cubes that double as the scenery – can grab people's attention, so can props in real life. For example, how often have you heard someone describe a match like this: 'It was a great goal, honestly. Imagine this beer mat was the goal keeper and this glass here was the post ...'

In extreme cases, it might even be possible to carry props with you if something is very much your party. I know of more than one person, for example, who has aced a presentation with the help of Lego, fruit and Velcro (though not, thankfully, at the same time).

The point is, theatrical ideas work when you're telling stories but you *don't* have to turn yourself into a diva to pull them off. Here is a selection of activities and ideas that will help you put some theatrical magic into your stories with attention, structure and scale ... and yet still allow you to remain yourself.

Chaining together your random talking

To get you started, let's revisit an idea, then build on it. The random talking exercise in Chapter Four wasn't just designed to get people talking to a mirror about hurricanes or cherry pie. If you study the behaviour of confirmed communicators, one striking fact emerges. They may indeed chatter about a selection of seemingly unrelated circumstances. However, as if by magic, one topic seems to blend into another, punctuated smoothly by various asides and answers to questions.

However, if you listen even more carefully, certain golden phrases appear. They include: 'By the way'; 'That reminds me ...'; and 'It's the same sort of thing as ...'. Again, the list of these linking phrases is limited only by your imagination but they give effortless polish to your speech.

The first stage of this process is to combine your previous 'random talking' with linking subjects together. This exercise will enable you to do that.

Links

Make a list of all the possible phrases you can think of that could link two or more subjects together. Think of the list as an ongoing project, rather than a single exercise. Read over your list from time to time, so that they spring to mind automatically.

The random dozen

Write a list containing at least twelve random subjects.

1. Your task (again, either in front of the mirror or with a friend) is to talk for at least a minute on six of the topics on the list, linking the topics together with five different phrases. Don't choose your six subjects in advance, just as they seem to pop into your mind. Don't worry about pauses and repetition. Just keep going for six minutes.

2. Hint. If the thought of this exercise makes you feel less confident than you do at your best, repeat the belief change exercise in Chapter One before you start.

Knowing when to stop

If you are not used to speaking up in social situations, it may seem odd to consider when you should *stop* doing so. However, as you become more and more fluent at socialising, you may also need to become more aware of when to stop. As you may have spent a lifetime up to this point listening patiently to others, thinking, 'I wish he or she would shut up and give me a chance to say something,' this is not a point to labour. Just be aware that, if people's eyes glaze over, they seem to be trying to escape or they join the conversation, perhaps with an adventurous cough or 'Uh ...', it might actually be time to stop, or at least pause to let other people have a turn.

Just in case you think that this would never happen to you, here's a cautionary tale. I once helped someone who was so shy that he was virtually monosyllabic. A few months and some social confidence later, he was so pleased to be able to tell stories to anyone who would listen that I actually heard one of his colleagues muttering, 'X never shuts up any more, does he?'

Of course, if you already love talking and are just reading this material to gain even more finesse, take careful note of this paragraph and remember the old adage: less is more.

Once upon a time: the role of imagination

Whether you considered yourself a 'natural talker' prior to this course or not, the skills of a true storyteller involve far more than just linking subjects together. That will give you a sense of flow but it may or may not sustain people's interest.

In order to get in the mood to do that, go back to your childhood or to bedtime stories with children in your family. Don't be afraid to feel the magic that runs through that phrase, 'Once upon a time'. It has been in use, in various forms, for thousands of years, long before Walt Disney or even the Brothers Grimm brought it to millions.

It may seem sacrilegious to ask how this magic manifests itself. However, this information, used and practised, will turn you into a master storyteller. As a start, consider these two monologues. In both cases, the speaker is talking about their last holiday. The question is, which of them do you find more interesting and why?

Story One

'Yeh, I enjoyed it. It was nice. Been there a couple of times with my partner. We were lucky, of course. The weather was good, like the food and the hotel. Met a few interesting people, too … Didn't really want to come back.'

Story Two

'You'll never guess where we went this year … Yeh [mentions place]. We'd been there before but I enjoyed it so much more this time … The weather was all warmth and balmy breezes. From the hotel, you could see a vast expanse of blue water in the bay. It seemed very, very deep and sparkled in the sun like diamonds on a moving carpet. Every evening, the hotel laid on an enormous buffet with fragrant rice, chicken wings, piles and piles of succulent fruit. You should have seen one of the guys staying there, he was such a character. He had this really strange clipped speech and wore slippers all the time but he turned out to have made a big fat fortune in mining, or so he said. It was great. Well, I expect you can tell why we didn't want to come back.'

When you have considered what it is that differentiates the two stories, keep reading, for a (nonexhaustive list) of storytelling tips.

It's likely that you found the second tale more interesting. Admittedly, it is slightly longer than the first. However, given the number of techniques used in the second one, it is, in fact, relatively compact and succinct. Stay calm. This does not mean that every single one of these techniques must be used each time in order to recount a story effectively. Just be aware that each of these tools is at your disposal, should you need them.

Hook people in

Look, first of all, at the way in which each speaker begins the story. In the second story, 'You'll never guess …' instantly draws in the attention of the listener, whereas 'Yeh …' does not quite achieve the same result. Other similar hooks to carry in your memory also include, 'Do you want to know something interesting?', and the simple 'Listen …'.

Audience participation

A useful storytelling trick is to find ways in which the audience becomes actively engaged in the tale. In a sense, the first story does this as there is so little detail that, if the listener cares to do so, they may wonder, for example, what the hotel was like.

However, the audience participation factors in the second case are more subtle. 'You'll never guess …' sets the pace in this respect and is followed by the invitation of 'I expect you can tell …' further on.

In addition, there is space for people to ask their own questions internally. The speaker pauses after the words 'I enjoyed it so much more this time …' almost as if she or he were giving the listener time to ask themselves why.

Using the senses

In order to involve the listener even more, it is likely that the speaker in the second case is right inside their own story. By this, I mean that if we were able to read his or her mind, we would find that they were actually re-living the entire experience, so that all the sights (such as the blue sea), sounds (of clipped speech), feelings (of balmy breezes), tastes (of succulent fruit), and smells (of fragrant rice) of the holiday destination are vividly evoked.

Details

In a sense, many of the reasons for giving details have been given above: they help to give the kind of sensory information that makes people feel involved. But details do not have to be solely sensory. They can also give an indication of other descriptions, for example, the reference to the tourist's slippers.

		CONCEPT		
		To describe something wonderful	To describe ways of obtaining information	To describe unpleasant object or situation
SENSE	Sight	It glowed	He saw	It was murky
	Smell	It had the smell of success	He got wind of it	It stank of
	Sound	It resonated	She heard	It was discordant
	Taste	It was 'flavour of the month'	She got a	It was not anyone's cup of tea
	Movements, Sensations and Feelings	It stood out	He felt	It was rough

The only caveat is that you can have too much detail. Had the story, for example, contained the complete list of all 28 items on the menu, plus a detailed description of the way in which the tables were laid, the listener might have decided that overkill had taken place.

Repetition

Even in the second story, there is relatively little repetition other than that the sea looked 'very, very deep' and there were 'piles and piles' of fruit. If the story were longer, there might well be a place for greater repetition. This has the effect of giving the listener a feeling of regularity and security within the tale. Just think of the average joke. Be cautious here, however. Repetition can be hypnotic and send people off into their own world. However, if that is your intention with a particular story, that's great but it may not be the best way to persuade your potential new client just how much you would energise their workforce. Choose the right tools for the job.

Direct speech

Quoting people while you tell a story gives your narrative tremendous power. Your listeners feel that they are meeting the characters in your story, especially if you can approximate their way of speaking at the same time. However, even if you can't, remembering their words is likely to be enough. Even from the extract of the second story, it's clear that 'big fat fortune' is not a phrase the speaker would be likely to use.

Humour

Entire books have been written on the role of humour in society and how to convey it. All that can be said generally, is that it is a very individual concept. Therefore, it may be better if you can inject a mild degree of humour into most of your socialising, rather than saving up your pet joke especially for the boss. Otherwise, you may just find either, that they have already heard 'the one about the three-legged toad', or that, for some inexplicable reason, they don't find it funny. Having said that, jokes, told judiciously, can make excellent conversational stories in themselves, so use your instincts.

If you do decide to take the approach of spicing your conversation with humour, how do you achieve this? In general, the safest course is to develop an eye and an ear for those details that will make other people laugh happily, without causing offence. For example, the second story includes a detail about the man's slippers. If he had been forced always to wear them to hide his grossly deformed feet, many people would consider this offensive and, therefore, not funny. Again, it is just a question of choosing the appropriate tools.

Comparisons

What is meant by 'comparisons'? Basically, it's using what your English teacher would have called 'similes'. One thing is described as being *like* another. Moreover, such comparisons are a powerful way of communicating your internal representation of a story to other people. In the second tale, a comparison is lurking in the phrase where the water 'sparkled in the sun *like* diamonds on a moving carpet'.

Now, some people may feel that such comparisons are flowery, perhaps even pompous and that's fine. The point is that they are another tool that is available to you, especially if you are in an environment that calls for more dramatic or colourful storytelling.

Making comparisons

1. On a piece of paper, write down and number four random objects or subjects.

2. Fill in the appropriately numbered words in the table below:

(1) _____	is like (2) _____	because _____ _____ _____ _____
(3) _____	is like (4) _____	because _____ _____ _____ _____

3. Now, fill in the two boxes in the third column, as imaginatively as you can. So for example, if the four words were 'doughnut, paperclip, memo, photo', you might pick out 'doughnut' and 'memo' and put, 'This doughnut is like my boss's memo because it's stodgy and goes round in a circle'.

4. Finally, put the same words in their new position in the grid opposite and repeat step three.

You should find that this exercise makes you much more creative and comfortable using metaphors and similes.

(4) _____	is like (2) _____	because _____ _____ _____
(1) _____	is like (3) _____	because _____ _____ _____

Delivery

We've touched on this already, in that pausing gives listeners time to ask internal questions and, therefore, engage in the story. In addition, though, it also gives time for information to sink into other people's consciousness, thus increasing your personal impact. Other delivery points that do the same thing include:

- Your pace, which should be varied and appropriate to the subject. (You might talk about scuba diving more calmly than white-water rafting, for example.)

- Your volume, which, again, should vary (quiet footsteps call for less sound than a brass band).

- Your tone. Match the emotion in your story with your tone of voice as far as you can. So, for example, the tone of the people talking about their holidays in this section should have been as happy and buoyant as possible.

True expression

1. Watch on TV or listen to a recording of an actor or speaker reciting a particular speech, story or poem. Listen to it and notice how they vary their pace, tone and volume.

2. Try this yourself by telling a story, joke or reciting a poem with as much expression in your volume, pace and tone as you can. (You can choose to recite or to speak off the top of your head here. It doesn't matter, as long as you concentrate on your volume, pace and tone.)

3. If you wish, you could try this in front of a friend or relative and ask them which they prefer.

4. If you find that your tone is still a little flat, experiment with imagining that the things you describe are actually happening to you, rather than simply being words you're reading from the page.

Notice at the end how much more confident you feel about storytelling.

Everyday stories

'This is great,' you might say, 'but my life is just not interesting enough to include any stories. I get up and look after the kids/go to work/whatever, then I go back to bed before it all begins again. What's exciting about that?'

You've already seen how a relatively simple event, like a holiday, can make an engaging story. Consider many of the works of published authors: people like Bill Bryson make their living just from observing small details in real life and weaving the results into an entertaining tale.

If you need any more proof, I must confess that I haven't had a particularly exciting day while writing this chapter, tapping away and watching a cat on the windowsill of the house opposite. But there was also nearly a bust-up that anyone could relate to, involving a call centre, a website and a very long wait with a happy ending. (You see, it doesn't take much to start a story.)

So, if you're new to spotting the stories or anecdotes in your life, the next exercises are especially for you. In the meantime, well, I hope you all live happily ever after … or happily enough to read the next chapter, anyway.

Spot the anecdote

Each day for the next week, make a point of spotting potential anecdotes in your life. You could note an interesting incident in the street, or a conversation in a shop. By the end of each day, you should have at least two incidents that could be recounted in an interesting way to someone else.

For example, say that you get up late, rush, put on your clothes quickly and lock yourself out. At first glance, this is just plain annoying, but told in the right way, it can make a great anecdote. It will give you the consolation at the time that at least you'll be able to laugh about it later as you tell everyone, '*and* it wasn't 'til I was halfway down the street that I realised my top was inside out' (trust me, I've done it).

If it helps, make notes at the end of each day, to help you remember relevant details.

Even after the week is over, make a habit of searching your life for recountable stories: they are everywhere.

Story time

Your task, at some time during the next week, is to take one of the anecdotes you noticed for 'Spot the anecdote' and actually incorporate it into a conversation with someone else, without telling them what you are doing. The conversation can be on the phone or in person. The only rule is that you must use as many storytelling techniques within it as you can.

Having done this, you'll be ready to try it out at a particular event, which is the subject of the next chapter.

Chapter Seven

Get Ready ...

It's time to give yourself a big pat on the back. You've got a huge range of ideas under your belt now and you've brushed up your skills and confidence several times over. Now it's also time to put it all together in an order that works for you and your life and to iron out any more inner and outer wrinkles that may still be in your way.

Finding an occasion

Many of you may already be roaring ahead with plans to party and you may have bought this book to boost the number of events you attend, just as much as to improve your feelings about them. So, if your diary is looking a bit blank, it could be because you're always drowned in work or caring responsibilities, or any of a mass of activities with which our lives can get crammed. What can you do about it?

The first step is to be really honest with yourself and work out why your social life may need a boost. Think of this as a positive exercise that will turbo-charge your social life. The reasons can vary wildly and are usually connected to your environment, habits and the beliefs you used to hold about your social life. Because you have had the habit of holding those beliefs for such a long time, it can take a short while for you to be aware of the hard evidence that your social tide has turned. But turn it will and you can help yourself to make this happen even faster.

If your social life hasn't had as much energy behind it as you would have liked, you may well have been following one of three common patterns. These are meant as a general guide only, so trust yourself as to the description or course of action that suits you best. Once detected, these patterns are easy to change. Even if you have a diary that other people might dream about, give the next few paragraphs some attention. They may shed some light on other parts of your life, or help you point someone else in a different direction if they ask.

The Blocker

You can spot the Blocker a mile off. Always busy, they don't have a blank space in their diary; it's just always full of tasks relating to work or other responsibilities. We're not talking social functions here either. If a Blocker works outside the home, they can be found beavering away on that oh-so-important administration, when all his or her co-workers have disappeared to the pub on a Friday night. They may also need to be restrained from actually coming into the office at the weekend.

A friend of mine used to be the PA of a renowned Blocker and she used to dread Monday mornings. While her co-workers were gently acclimatising themselves back into the office, she would be greeted upon arrival (of course, her boss turned up by 8am each morning) with a pile of freshly produced work, as a result of his weekend labours.

Blocking doesn't have to evolve from paid work, either. Another Blocker I once knew was convinced that, although she did get some respites from caring for her elderly parents, they should be used solely for sensible purposes, such as shopping. This was despite the fact that her responsibilities weighed her down considerably and often caused her to snap in front of her parents in a way that she might not have done had she allowed herself a little gentle socialising to oil the wheels of her life.

So, what's really going on here? There are, of course, no hard-and-fast rules and every individual is different. However, a Blocker tends to be using their responsibilities as a shield to avoid socialising. In the first case, my friend's boss had been badly hurt in a long-term relationship. This made him prefer to spend time in the office, rather than put himself in a situation where he might be hurt again. In turn, being office bound had become a habit, long after the wounds caused by his previous relationship had healed. There is a famous maxim that states that work tends to expand to fill the time available. Therefore, if no time is set aside for having fun, your responsibilities may conspire to help you become a Blocker. In the second example, the daughter was painfully aware of her responsibilities to others, to an extent where they swamped her duty to herself.

However, if you recognised yourself in these character sketches, there are many available options. One of my favourites is particularly simple and does not involve you shirking any responsibilities. After all, it is likely to have been your conscientious nature that led you to 'block' in the first place.

1. The first stage to remember is that you have individual value just as you are. Therefore, your first responsibility is to honour that value. If you're unsure about this, consider what I would call the Oxygen Mask Principle. This comes from airline safety drills, in which the cabin staff always stress that, 'in the event of oxygen masks becoming necessary, you should ensure that your own mask is securely fitted before attempting to help others'. So, allow yourself to get used to the idea that socialising, like other forms of enjoyment, is part of the emotional oxygen that you need in order to be able to fulfil your responsibilities to others more effectively.

2. Next, make sure that at least ten per cent of your free time in any given week is allocated to having fun, whatever that means to you, whether at parties and events or elsewhere. Put it in your diary along with other appointments, so that

you actually get to give it priority and do it. If, for some reason, you can't fill the time with something that you'd consider to be fun (which should be very much the exception rather than the rule), make a pact with yourself that the time has to be spent doing absolutely nothing.

The Witholder

Do you have colleagues or acquaintances who, even though they seem pleasant enough in general conversation, never really divulge anything about themselves? If you ask them to join you for coffee, they may accept but then back out or, even more likely, refuse your offers so often that you cease to make them. You might work with them for years and yet never really get the feeling that you know them. They may be Witholders.

The issue of Witholders can be a thorny one. When I mention it, people sometimes mistakenly think that I am advocating a lack of personal privacy, or that they should be forced to tell everyone they meet about their wife's Caesarean. On the contrary, levels of personal privacy vary greatly and, as we'll see in the next chapter, the amount that is divulged will change according to the occasion.

A true Witholder is keeping back, not just their information but their actual participation in an event. So, even when you do get them to come to an event, they may answer all your questions politely and fluently (for there is more to this than shyness) but their answers will be short and eliciting further information is like pulling teeth.

So, what's going on in the mind of a Witholder? Again, there are no hard-and-fast rules but, in general, the benefit they gain from withholding is likely to be a sense of security. For whatever reason, they view most people with suspicion, thinking, 'What does he/she *really* want from me?' They find it hard to believe that people may simply want their presence and fear giving away too much because any information or emotional reaction might be used against them at a later date. Then, when friends and acquaintances begin to drop away, Witholders console themselves with the thought that, secretly, this was just the kind of breach of trust they had been predicting all along.

So, if you're socialising with a Witholder, or think that you might err towards that pattern of behaviour yourself, what steps might you take to make progress?

1. If you want a Witholder at your party, give them plenty of notice of the event. Respect their need to keep their own counsel and resist the temptation to badger them for extra information. Also, even if they refuse your invitations, keep offering them for far longer than you would to anyone else. Your consistency will be appreciated and is part of the trust-building exercise that will help a Witholder to trust you. You will also receive a huge benefit, because Witholders' natural sense of discretion makes them loyal and trustworthy friends.

2. If you yourself want to withhold less, here's a two-pronged approach to enable you to make the change smoothly:

    (a) Just allow yourself to imagine what your social life would be like if you could trust other people easily. How would you think, feel and behave? Promise yourself that, next time you socialise (and this event can be as simple as a chat at the shops or the coffee machine), you will act as though you assume that everyone is trustworthy, even if this feels unfamiliar at first. Afterwards, allow yourself to reflect on the difference that your new approach made to your attitude and success. If it helps you to capture the new feelings, write them down in a diary or notebook.

    (b) Next time you socialise or have any interaction with another person, concentrate particularly on what you can give to that interaction. If you find your thoughts straying to what the other person might be taking from you, or what they might be 'out to get', just gently but firmly return your concentration to what you can give. You may like to record your successes in your notebook, as above.

The Sorter

The chief characteristic of the Sorter is that he or she rules themselves out of social occasions because of their own preconceptions. These can take two seemingly opposite forms. How often have you heard people say, 'Oh, I'm not going to that because they're not my sort of people'? Now, it's possible that the speaker has reached this conclusion by careful consideration of their social style (see below) and concluded that the discomfort outweighs the potential benefit. But it is far more likely that they are thinking of a variation on one of the following two themes:

'I'm not good/popular/clever enough to mix with people like that'

OR

'I'm *too* good/popular/clever to mix with people like that'

In both cases above, the effect is to limit the scope of the person's social life.

Sorters bring us around to another issue that is often swept under the carpet: status. Before we go on to look at how Sorters can expand their options, let's nail the question of status once and for all. Thankfully, we have moved away from the times when a person was judged overtly by their accent, schooling or their parents' jobs. Yet, many human beings still feel a need to establish rank. In America, which has long-boasted that it is the 'land of the free', try getting an invitation to the Oscars if you happen not to be one of the glitterati.

Fortunately, there is a way out of the maze. If you bear in mind one key point, you'll be able to glide around any issues of status or class and have fun, quite literally, any time, any place, anywhere: equality is the real issue. If you truly believe that you are equal to (not, better, worse or the same as but *equal to*) anyone else, then you can go anywhere with ease. Let others worry about sorting and forming cliques if they wish. You don't have to subscribe to their views, even though they are perfectly free to hold them. So, how would you set about embodying this belief? There are two golden rules:

1. *Remember rapport.* As we saw a few chapters ago, by aligning yourself with others' physical actions, turns of phrase and other characteristics, you pay them the compliment of respecting where they are. You can then lead them in any direction you wish, preserving your own sense of identity and re-affirming your confidence.

2. Once rapport is established, *be yourself.* If there is one common denominator among truly happy partygoers, it is their ability to take pride in being themselves. Remember, I once met a most charming millionaire who delighted in wearing slippers at all times. To take a more famous example, Emma Hamilton, the famous mistress of Lord Nelson, was apparently always more than happy to talk about her time as a servant whenever the topic came up.

However, status isn't just a concept for the wealthy or privileged. It is a state of mind and this means that it is available to anyone. If you believe you are worthy, then no one can take this away from you. Equally, other people are less likely to treat you with respect if you do not value yourself. The rest of this chapter will give you the tools you need to pinpoint precisely how you can achieve this state most easily.

Undervaluation

Getting back to our Sorters, what can you do if you have formed the habit of undervaluing yourself? How can you feel resourceful enough, not only to turn up at an event but to enjoy it? Actually, if you feel valuable, then other people will automatically treat you as such (it is less of an effort to take you at your own worth than to conduct a detailed question-and-answer session during an event). However, this is rather a chicken-and-egg scenario: you need the secret of your own worth before you can demonstrate it to others. Otherwise, however much other people praise you, the impact of the praise may stay with you only briefly, before draining away, rather like running a bath without putting in the plug. The following ideas will help you to recover your sense of worth if it seems to have gone missing.

Your beliefs

1. If you have identified some specific beliefs relating to your sense of worth, revisit Chapter One of this book and go through the belief change exercises in the light of them.
2. Make particularly sure that you have convinced yourself of your own equality in the previous exercise. If it is challenging, act as if it were true for a few days or weeks and notice the difference.

Your talents

There are, I guarantee, certain things that you do that no one else in the entire world does better. Unusual though it may seem, just allow yourself the time to write down five of them in the space below (or elsewhere).

1 _____

2 _____

3 _____

4 _____

5 _____

Whenever you feel the stirrings of any lack of confidence, switch your thoughts and concentrate on one of these talents until, one day soon, your core belief will be in your own abilities.

The little things

However grand they may appear, there are certain everyday tasks that all human beings must carry out in order to stay healthy and alive. These include washing, cleaning their teeth, eating and, yes, going to the toilet. If at any time you feel yourself to be in awe of any other person, just imagine them carrying out one of these tasks.

On the other side of the coin ...

Suppose you are sometimes a Sorter who tends to exclude others, you can do this as well as, at the same time, undervaluing yourself.

Benefits

If you do find yourself saying things like, 'I'm better than them,' just ask yourself, 'What benefit will I gain from taking this approach?' This is not a trick question: the length of your resulting list will surprise you.

Often, people who exclude others out of fear, or for similar reasons to undervaluers, do so because of a lack of confidence and a perceived need to protect their position. Conversely, some of the most genuinely popular people, such as the late Princess of Wales, gain their popularity by their willingness to reach out to many different kinds of people.

Concentrating on the best in other people

For the next week, make a point of homing in on the talents of every person that you meet. You may well notice other factors that are part of your normal assessment process, such as dress or speech patterns but do your best to put them to one side and concentrate solely upon the person's talent(s).

Repeat this exercise during all social interactions, whether party-based or not. Make notes on the changes in your perception in your notebook, if this helps you to remember them.

Shyness

You may have noticed that I haven't included a category for people who feel they are simply shy or awkward. That's because, if you follow the exercises in this book carefully and consistently, it's likely that these feelings will no longer feature in your life as they once did.

What's more, it's almost certain that your previous years of shyness have left you with an acute sense of empathy for others, as well as observational skills that will entertain naturally louder and probably less observant people.

Filling your diary

So, now that you've cleared the way, you're ready to fill your diary but only so much as to still give it the very best of your energy. How do you do that? As always, of course, there are no set rules. You will probably find it helpful to start small and work upwards. This will allow you to pace yourself so that you adapt easily and naturally to a social life that is tailored to your own definition of success.

Also, as the saying goes, 'From little acorns, mighty oak trees grow,' so be aware of every opportunity to interact with others, whether on the phone, saying hello in passing, or even by e-mail. Once you have done this consistently for a few weeks and incorporated the other tips mentioned earlier, people will begin to take it as read that you are a sociable person who would be an asset at any gathering. When they reach this conclusion, the invitations will roll in.

Ideas for getting invites

If your diary's looking more empty than you'd like, here are the top ways to fill it with activities you'll actually enjoy.

1. Ask for an invite.

> This may sound obvious, but often if you hear something mentioned by someone and you say, 'Oh, I'd love to come,' they will invite you.
>
> But what if they're only doing it out of politeness? Isn't it rude? Well, not necessarily. There are dozens of reasons why someone might have wanted to invite you. From the point of view of a person inviting you, they may, for all you know, have a worry that not enough people will come, and be delighted that you've asked to

come along. They may have wanted to ask you all along, but have feared rejection, or felt that they don't know you well enough. They may just not have known that you were interested in coming along.

Certainly, if confidence has been an issue for you, and you're serious about being more forthcoming, you might like to experiment with this. After turning up to a couple of things at which you feared you might not be welcome, and having a good time, your confidence will grow.

As we're in the business of bringing out your 'life and soul' here, though, an extra point that ensures you'll always be welcome, and invited back, is to express the reason for your interest and the contribution you could make. Enthusiasm is much more important than expertise, 'Oooh, I love walking ... I didn't know you ran a rambling club' was enough to get someone I know a permanent invitation recently.

2. **Get on lists.**

    Yes, marketing lists can be really annoying when they only result in shiny paper on the doormat. But they're also a great source of invitations, sometimes to fairly classy free events that the sponsors put on to advertise themselves. They're all places to meet people, and maybe even people who share your interests, if the marketing departments or people running clubs and organisations have done their job well.

    Even if you choose to join more local groups, like clubs advertising in a library, local paper or regional Internet site, this method works. I know one person who went from having a blank diary apart from work, to being busy every weekend for three months, just by doing this.

3. **Throw a party or event yourself.**

    This idea works because of the reliable way in which people tend to give back that which they receive. And no, before you ask, it doesn't matter how long it is since you've been in touch with the people you invite, as invitations have this magical ability to re-forge connections, and to help you make new ones with all the extra people that your contacts are likely to want to bring along.

What sort of 'soul' is going to this party, anyway?

So, now that we have ensured that there will be a social occasion for which to prepare, where do you begin? A good starting point is to decide which environments, events and parties actually help you feel most comfortable in your own skin. Everybody has a different social character. Just as one person likes curry and the other prefers fish and chips, so one person's idea of heaven is a night down at the pub, while his neighbour prefers a black-tie dinner or clubbing. There are no right and wrong answers. There are only different preferences and each one of them will make you feel naturally comfortable in one environment and less so in another.

The trick is to know both your own preferences and the nature of the event you're thinking of attending in detail. Then you can see how closely the two match at any given time. So you need to be able to work out how to make choices that leave you feeling comfortable and good about yourself.

So, how do you achieve this feat? The next activity will guide you through every step of the process.

Your party preferences

1. Do this part of the activity very quickly. For each item in the left-hand column, write an example of it that appeals to you most in the central column. It doesn't matter whether or not the item is remotely linked to parties, events or socialising: it may well not be.

For instance, next to 'Activity', you might put walking, if that is what you enjoy. Leave the right-hand column blank for now. I have included an example of a completed table at the end of this activity.

Item	Your example	Reason
Activity		
Colour		
Item of clothing (owned by you)		
Food		
Drink		
Song/piece of music		
Aroma or scent		
Way of relaxing		
Film of RV programme		
Conversation topic		
Person you most admire		
Season		
Place		
Time of day		

2. Now write down a *possible* reason for each of your choices in the right-hand column. Again, it is important that you give your instinctive response, so just write them in as quickly as you can.

3. Next, study your responses in the right-hand column more closely. Which common factors link each, or many of your choices? (For instance, if you like orange because it is a warm colour, this might link with a response that said 'Summer' was your favourite season, if the reason for that choice was high temperature. You could express this link in a variety of ways, just one of which might be 'heat').

4. Be creative when making your links. When you have as many of them as possible, but at least three, list them in the space below.

   i) _____

   ii) _____

   iii) _____

   _____

   _____

5. Finally, ask yourself, what person, place or thing combines all the qualities you've isolated at stage four? This is a highly individual choice. For instance, one person may be drawn to things that are, say, 'lively', 'colourful' and 'playful' and choose 'carnival', whereas someone else might decide that the thing that represents 'lively', 'colourful' and 'playful' most for them is a kaleidoscope.

6. Then write down (or draw) your chosen symbol here _____

At this moment, the symbol represents you as the life and soul of the party you'd most naturally choose. Remember also that your style will change as you do, so do repeat this exercise every few months and note the developments.

Example

Item	Your example	Reason
Activity	Neighbours' New Year party	Local and friendly
Colour	Red	Vibrant
Item of clothing (owned by you)	Jeans	Casual, comfy
Food	Chips	Informal
Drink	Tea	Comforting
Song/piece of music		
Aroma or scent	Vanilla	Sweet
Way of relaxing	Going to cinema	Local, intimate
Film of RV programme	Comedy	Relaxing
Conversation topic	Friends	Familiar
Person you most admire	My brother	Always good for a laugh
Season	Winter	Cosy
Place	Forests	Protected, natural
Time of day	Evening	Social

The person who filled in these answers would be likely to have a symbol that was also relaxing, cosy, familiar and protective, such as a teddy bear. It would follow from this that they might not enjoy formal events, but might really enjoy a party in the neighbourhood, or a barbecue in the garden.

Knowing your natural party style is important in a number of ways. First, it helps you remain true to yourself, providing a touchstone with which to identify, should you choose to do so. Second, it can act as a pointer as to which inner resources you may need to approach an event with the greatest possible confidence. Third, it gives you a baseline from which to calculate any adjustments you may need to make in order to feel comfortable. As a final bonus, it'll also make it easier for you to choose between two events (given that your new-found status as the life and soul of the party is sure to boost the number of invitations of all kinds that you receive).

Stretching yourself versus false behaviour

So, if it's easiest to be the life and soul at those parties that resonate with the *real* you, what should you do about the ones you have to go to but don't enjoy? Should you just decline with a shrug and a casual, 'Oh, no thank you ... Your party's just not in line with my soul, you know'? That's probably not the greatest way to retain friends, never mind make more!

And where do you draw the line between discomfort with the whole idea of interacting and genuine unease at the thought of a particular event that really isn't you? Here are some guidelines that may help you make the best decision in all circumstances, every time.

Parties are supposed to be fun

Try this golden rule: if it feels uncomfortable, STOP. Parties and other events are supposed to be fun so, if something isn't fun by its very nature, you're most unlikely to be the life and soul of that gathering, in which case, find a way round them. Offer to meet relevant people elsewhere, or get someone else to go.

However, it may well be that the reasons for attending a particular event are worth making the effort to stretch yourself and your confidence just a little further. There is a huge difference between the temporary feeling of discomfort you may encounter when embarking on something new, and choosing to change your approach to existing events and being left with the lingering sense of unease you feel when you are not true to yourself. To be aware of which is which, run through the following quick exercise.

What feels right to you?

1. Think back to a time when you felt uncomfortable and, looking back, that discomfort sprang from some situation or activity being 'just not you'. Recall that time in as much sensory detail as possible. What do you see, hear, touch, taste, smell and feel inside as you think about the experience? Note down your impressions.

2. Now think back to a time when, although you felt some temporary discomfort, the benefit of hindsight tells you that the discomfort lifted and paved the way for greater success or other positive experiences. Bring that back to mind in as much sensory detail as you did the previous experiences.

3. Now compare the two experiences and note down the key points of each. For example, lingering discomfort may have been heavier for you than the discomfort of moving outside your usual sphere of activity into something new.

This process gives you a yardstick by which you can judge whether a nervous reaction in relation to a social event is due to understandable caution or a deeper sense of unease about an event sitting uncomfortably with your sense of identity.

Assuming that the particular event you have in mind is causing you to feel sick at the thought of expanding your comfort zone, how can you overcome this? One option is, as the majority of people may advise you, simply to crash through your nervousness. However, as socialising should be an easy and enjoyable process, how about approaching the event in an easy and enjoyable manner as well?

The first step is to start thinking about the event in a new way. For example, say that your nervousness is causing you to consider refusing an invitation, even though you know that the event could, in fact, be fun and lead you on to even greater success. Consider this: you could tell yourself that, in the long run, passing up an opportunity to do something new is a way of being untrue to yourself. If, in the past, you have turned down invitations simply because the people offering them were outside your usual sphere and comfort zone, then you may have denied yourself access to new friends and fresh opportunities and, consequently, prevented yourself from fulfilling your full potential at that time.

The crucial point is to use this new insight as a lesson for the future, rather than an opportunity for self-recrimination. Now that the tide of your beliefs has turned, it's the perfect time to revamp your feelings about the actual events, to support the changes you've already made in relation to other people and your social approach.

However, if this sounds familiar, all is well. Contrary to popular belief, it's never too late to change and to keep changing. The next set of opportunities is just around the corner, as close as your next social event, which could, in itself, be as simple as a conversation on a bus or train.

'No choice'

'This is all very well,' you may be thinking, 'but my next social event is *too* close. I'm dreading an event next week and I have absolutely no choice about going. My symbol is a pint of beer and the event is more like a glass of champagne. How do I go along, keep my sanity and still stay true to myself?'

First of all, you might find it helpful to consider whether you really, really *have* to go, or whether you are, in fact, choosing to go in order to avoid some other consequence. If so, which course of action is easier in the long run?

I know of a popular, active and sociable lady who really wants to have more free time at the weekends. Yet every weekend, she feels obliged to have her mother around for tea 'because she expects it and she's used to it, I can't disappoint her', which is effectively limiting her options. She loves her mother dearly but the real irony is that I know her mother as well and she has quite often said, 'I really enjoy going around [to her daughter's] for tea but I wish I didn't have to do it quite so often ... I have to turn down so many other invitations.' So, before you decide you really *have* to do something that feels restrictive, it's probably worth checking whether or not your assumption is still true.

In the same way, experiment with accepting or offering only those invitations about which you really feel positive. You might well be surprised by other people's reactions and help yourself move towards a more relaxing life at the same time, even though it may feel a little strange at first.

A couple of years ago, I was organising my birthday party. As it wasn't a landmark birthday, I decided to hold the event in my flat, which limited the available space. I recognised, of course, that not all the invited people would turn up but, even allowing for this, they would still have had to spill out into the street. So, in a desperate attempt to make space, I looked at the list again and asked myself, 'Who do I *really* want to invite?'

The results of this one question astonished me and were far more profound than you might expect. First, there was sufficient space to accommodate my guests in the flat. Second, all the people whom I invited said an immediate 'yes' without the irritating 'I'll be able to let you know nearer the time' type of comment. Call me suspicious if you like but that just smacks of 'I'll come if I don't get a better offer'. That is fine and perfectly within the other person's right to say but a straight 'No, thank you' is so much more polite and easier to plan around. Third and last, there were no last-minute cancellations and we all had a great time. Cutting out the 'have tos', 'musts', 'got tos' and 'shoulds' made life easier and happier for everyone.

A silk purse ...

You have now conscientiously worked through your own reasons for not going to an event that you still need to attend. You feel as enthusiastic about it as a teetotaller at a wine tasting. Is it possible to make a silk purse out of what is, in your opinion, a social sow's ear? The answer is yes, provided that you hunt for the purse.

As we saw in the chapter on beliefs, people tend to get what they expect in their social life. Therefore, if you expect that your neighbour's party will be about as much fun as a trip to the dentist, then you'll be right. But if you really have to go, start looking for the positives before you even set out. Are any of their friends likely to tell entertaining stories? Even if they are of a different generation to you, can you learn something from them? Perhaps they have relations or acquaintances who may need your help or who might be able to help you. Possibly they always serve lovely food or have a welcoming house. Whatever the plus factors are, focus on them and refuse to allow yourself to think negatively. Both positive and negative thoughts multiply naturally, it's just that the positive ones tend to be more fun and make you feel more sociable.

Positive associations

1. Think of a forthcoming social event that does not make you feel good at the moment. If you can't think of a social event, any other event will also work.
2. Write down at least five positive associations you can make in your mind in relation to that event.

_____

_____

_____

_____

_____

3. Each time you think about the event from now on, allow yourself only to think positively about it. If further positive points spring to mind, add them to the list above.
4. If, on the other hand, you notice yourself thinking negatively about the event, keep feeling good about yourself. You are human and there are going to be some times when it's easier than others to think positively. So, whenever you find yourself thinking less than positively, simply acknowledge it and make a deliberate choice to replace any negative thoughts with positive ones.
5. This process can also be carried out during the event.
6. If you like, note down in your diary how the event went. I guarantee that, if you have followed this procedure, your feelings about the event will be very different to your earlier view.

Your outcome

Sometimes, we have a choice as to which events we can attend but, other times, there is no choice (as when Auntie Sue's cousin's daughter's wedding is taking place 400 miles away on a weekend when you'd rather be, well, anywhere else). In either case it's essential to know what your outcome is. If there is an element of choice, you may decide that this event is not for you. Often, once you know your outcome, the events that seemed mandatory can in fact become optional (after all, you haven't seen Auntie Sue for years, have you?). If there really is genuinely no choice in the situation, then at least you can make the best of the opportunity.

You may be surprised to read about choosing whether or not to attend a particular event. Surely, if you become a true partygoer, all occasions are fair game and useful, right? Wrong. Occasions that make you feel uncomfortable, despite your new role as the life and soul of the party, or for which you can see no point, are unlikely to enable you to shine. They might present an ideal occasion at which to practise your newly acquired skills, however, once you have mastered these, they can be a waste of valuable energy that, in our busy world, could be better spent elsewhere. What's more, if you do make a conscious and willing choice to go to a party or event, just the act of knowing that you made a considered choice to be there can make it much more fun for everyone.

How do you decide which events are worth your while? The first step is to get clear about your anticipated outcome. The next, should you decide to go to the event, is to establish a positive reason for going. This means that, not only should there be a reason for going (e.g. not being left out), but that the reason should be positively phrased. So, for example, the phrase 'to avoid being left out', should be changed to 'to join the others'. The exercise that follows will help you establish positive intentions more easily. The positive intention will be both much more enjoyable in itself and much more likely to help you have fun when the event arrives.

A few more instant confidence boosts

If you're already raring to go, you can skip this section and move straight on to the next chapter. If, however, there is still just a touch of uncertainty or nervousness when you think about a particular event, ease it out of your thoughts with the next exercise.

Often when people come to me for advice about how to socialise more easily, they readily admit that they are standing in their own way. Yet every time they try to catch hold of their nameless, shapeless fear, it eludes them. Sometimes, as with the lady whose fear of making conversation turned into a fear of walking into a room, a limiting belief can go underground in order to escape detection. Or, take the example of an executive who really could not understand the cause of his unease at business functions. He was one of the most egalitarian people I have ever met, yet could not get comfortable when socialising with his bosses. Like many people, it turned out that some of his experiences at school were still spilling over into his working life, 30 years later. Defences that served him well then were long-redundant but continued to operate, until he found them and was able to switch them off. How did he do this? He carried out the next activity and, like many people, found a whole new level of confidence in the process.

If either this transfer of fears, or their being a complete mystery, rings any bells with you, then the next activity will help you dig just that little bit deeper in order to make changes more easily. It may seem novel but, as many people will vouch, it really does work.

Resource yourself

1. Find a quiet place, with plenty of space, where you can remain undisturbed for at least twenty minutes.

2. Imagine that your entire life – past, present and future – can be represented by a line.

3. In your mind, lay that line down on the floor. Ensure that the space you choose to visualise it is free from obstacles right along its length.

4. Choose a spot on the line that represents the present, then go and stand in it.

5. While standing in the present, facing the future, recall any negative emotions you feel as you think about social events, or one particular event.

6. Close your eyes and walk backwards until you reach the time in your life when this emotion first arose. Trust me and yourself. You will know the right point at which to stop. How old were you at that time or how old might you have been? What's going on in your life at that time? What can you see, hear, feel, touch, taste and smell? What are you saying? Is anyone else around? If so, who?

7. Check that this was the first occasion when you felt that feeling by walking even further back and noticing whether or not it is still there. If it is, repeat step six.

8. Open your eyes and step off your line, so that it is now in front of you going from right to left or left to right.

9. From this new position, what advice would you give to your younger self? What resources did you need then that you have acquired since?

10. When you have identified the advice or resources, step back into the present on the line. For each resource or piece of advice in turn, think about an occasion when you really felt you had mastered it, or were utilising your advice or resources effectively. Get into the mood of the event as much as you can through sights, sounds, feelings, tastes and smells. When the mood is at its height, turn round and communicate this to the younger you in whatever way seems appropriate. For example, you might 'beam it back', or 'talk' to your younger counterpart.

11. Step off the line again.

12. Rejoin the line as your younger self.

13. Experience the benefit of your new resources. Draw in even more of them if you need or want to.

14. Then, walk forward along the line into the present, with the benefit of those new resources.

15. Check that now, as you face the future, you are feeling positive about parties and social events. If, by any chance, you think you could feel even better, repeat this activity from step six until you do.

16. Walk forward into your future on the line, to the next social event and even beyond, with the benefit of your new resources.

17. Finish the activity back in the present then step off the line. If this method works for you, write down your impressions.

In this chapter, you've been clearing any and all remaining blocks to going out there and really enjoying yourself as the life and soul of any party. Turn the page to link up all your ideas and turn them into an action plan that'll work for you.

Chapter Eight

Get Set ...

As you saw earlier in relation to Olympic athletes, 90 per cent of all action can actually be made more accurate and effective if you give it prior thought. Therefore, if you treat this chapter as a mental rehearsal in all senses, you will be 90 per cent of the way to being the life and soul of the party, even before you put a foot out of your own door.

In this chapter, you will be giving some thought to the practical issues you may need to think about in advance, then putting everything together in a final, mental dress rehearsal.

Party checklist

Here's a brief rundown of the kind of issues you might want to think about before any party or social event.

Timing

There are two schools of thought on timing: 'fashionably late' and 'on the button'. My husband and I seem to take opposite views on this every time.

In truth, though, how you manage the timing is going to depend very much on the event you're going to and your own circumstances. For example, it might be a very laid-back affair where you suspect no one will turn up before 10pm. However, if you've got transport issues or a babysitter and you want to get to the party at all, then your strategy is probably going to involve turning up earlier.

It is also possible that you may be one of those people who feel that they're always running late. In fact, one of my friends once demonstrated this by managing to arrive at a party we held, ten minutes after the last of the other guests had gone (and yes, we did let him in and re-ignite the party in his honour). If this rather extreme example strikes a chord with you, there's a simple solution. Do what radio DJs, TV presenters and trainers do and 'backtime'. If you start off knowing the time you need to leave before you set out, you calculate all the timings backwards from that point. By thinking, for example, 'I have to leave by 11pm, so if I want to spend two hours there, I'll need to arrive by 9pm, which means leaving here at 8.30 or 8.15 if I want to factor in some contingency time,' will ensure you don't miss the fun.

'I've got nothing to wear'

Stereotypically, this is a female cry but, as clothes and class distinctions melt away, maybe none of us is saying this, or caring about it as people did in the past. The golden rule is to make sure you are going to feel comfortable in whatever you put on, both physically and emotionally. Think about this in relation to your natural style, discussed a few chapters back, if you'd like some extra ideas.

Occasionally, there will be times when it can be useful to check in advance what you are expected to wear, fancy dress parties being cases in point. As so many people will happily go to one of these, as long as they don't actually have to dress up, be really sure of your ground if you take the plunge, even if you're a natural, roaring extrovert. I have a friend who is one of the most outward going people I know but even she admits that it was hard to feel like the life and soul of the party when she turned up at a fancy dress in full hired skirts and ruffles, only to discover that everyone else had opted for jeans and jumpers.

Flirting

If you're one of those people who think parties were made for flirting, you can probably skip on down to the next heading. But if the very word fills you with horror and dread, here's some serious consolation.

First of all, it doesn't work in every environment. Would you really want to get your next promotion because you listened to the CEO in a sensual way? Or, would Great-Uncle Wilfred's funeral *really* be a comfortable place to 'pull' or, indeed, to worry too much about whether you were the life and soul of the party in the first place?

Second, even if you are going to a 'flirt-friendly' setting, remember this really encouraging fact. *Most other people can't flirt either.* Plus, they really want everyone else just to be genuine and pleasant. When you think about it, it makes sense. Say you *are* looking for 'the one' and you put lots of effort into putting up a flirtatious front that's not really you. For one thing, nonflirty people might be deterred from speaking to you. For another, you might actually hook up with someone, only for you both to discover that it doesn't work down the line, because the real you is a different person.

Third, if you *really*, really still want to learn to flirt, there are people who can teach you how to do so in a more genuine way and you'll find their details at the end of the book. In the meantime, you could always just experiment with being the real you, the life and soul of the party, your way and see what happens.

Networking

Of course, you may have bought this book for more business or career-orientated reasons. In which case, it won't be talk of flirting that interests you but networking. If I had a penny for every time someone wanted tips about networking. So many people seem to think of it as a cold-blooded concept that, as this book is about life and *soul*, it seems a good place to point out that networking, in the sense that most people use it, simply doesn't work at all.

Just humour me for a minute and turn this on its head. If you were at an event and in some kind of position of power whether as a potential client, an employer or mentor, any of which you could have been at some point, how would *you* feel about the idea of being caught in someone's net? How would you feel if you were merely being viewed as someone in a room to be worked in another's pursuit of an ambition?

Contrast this with how much you might enjoy a friendly chat with an interesting person who brought life, soul and goodwill to the exchange? If their business card just happened to end up with you so that they could help you further or prolong the chat in the future, how different might that feel to being networked? Let me spell it out. Networking is something you do to computers, not people. Be the life and genuine soul of the party and opportunities will just happen, naturally.

Presence

'Presence' can be quite a buzzword for some people. Like charisma, everyone wants it but few people can define it. Of course, if you've made all the belief changes and practised all the skills so far, you'll be well on your way to projecting presence in your own personal style anyway. However, you can help to accentuate and accelerate the process and here's how.

Pick the most powerful of your new beliefs and 'shout' it loudly and forcefully inside your head as you enter a room or event where you most need to make a presence.

One naturally modest and self-effacing person I know decided to say to himself as he entered a room, sweeping it with his eyes for good measure, 'Who shall I choose to grace with my presence today?' Apparently, people commented on how much more confidence and presence he exuded as a result. He didn't tell them the secret and, just in case you're wondering, he became neither big-headed nor immodest as a result, just a lot more self-confident.

Final mental rehearsal

It may be best to approach this next activity in two stages. First, read it quickly, to get a general idea of that which is suggested and the various pieces of actual information contained within it. Then, you might like to read it more slowly again, thinking your way through your forthcoming event specifically as you do so. Repeat this stage as much as you need to.

First of all, find a quiet place, where you will not be disturbed for at least 15 minutes. Then, get comfortable. Just relax and allow yourself to consider the various stages of your forthcoming event and the success that it will be for you.

Next, think in as much detail and with as much feeling as possible about your new positive beliefs. Set off as many of your triggers as you need to in order for this to happen and allow yourself to imagine, once more, the way in which your social life will be different as a result of these new beliefs.

Reassure yourself that all your preparation is working its magic. See, hear, feel, touch, taste and smell every aspect and every stage of the event at which you want to shine. Let your imagination wander first of all to the point just before the event, where everything is in place and working well. You are experiencing it as if it's actually happening now.

You are in plenty of time and you are keen to begin. You have all the resources you need, both inside and outside. You have nothing to do other than enjoy yourself. What are you wearing, thinking and saying to yourself and others? How does that feel? Hold the feeling for as long as you can but for at least 30 seconds.

Now think of yourself arriving at the event. Will you want to make a grand entrance or not? In your imagination, you can run through several different scenarios. If the event is low-key and it is your natural social style or you make the choice to slip in unnoticed, you may envisage yourself melting seamlessly into a throng of inviting people. On the other hand, if you choose to make a bolder entrance, you may deliberately arrive later. Your appearance may be deliberately more striking, more colourful or stand out in some other way. If this is the case, as you enter the room this time, remind yourself that you are intending to attract attention at this event and that you are worth every single second of their time. Let any and all other positive thoughts and ideas also express themselves in your mind at this point.

Now it is time for you to decide on how you choose to approach this event in even more detail. If it is a smaller gathering, full of people you know well, perhaps you need do no more than settle into your natural social character. If the event you are thinking about is a bigger one, you may need to imagine yourself looking around the room, perhaps from a slightly elevated position, particularly if you are short. Be aware that you are smiling warmly at everyone and that, as you do so, all the resources that you have locked into that smile will come flowing through you. Know also that the people you most need to contact will seem to stand out as you look around and that you can easily and naturally engage with them in a way that's friendly, appropriate and fun for you both.

Perhaps your initial scan of the room will include walking around this imaginary event. If so, how does the setting change as you walk? Be aware that it would be especially effective to make your walk look as purposeful as possible, so keep your intentions for the event firmly in mind, your head up and your shoulders back. Whole crowds will part for a person who appears purposeful.

As you start to do this in your imagination, think also about your intentions for this event. What is your ideal outcome? Think about what it is that you want in precise detail. What will you be saying, doing, seeing and feeling when you achieve it? What will you be hearing and receiving from other people as you achieve it? Also, remind yourself why you personally want this outcome and why it is important. As you feel your desire and anticipation, remind yourself, now that you have set your course, you can afford just to relax and enjoy yourself. If you were to cling on to your intentions too tightly, they might not come back to you so easily. Just concentrate on being the genuine you.

As you start to approach groups and individuals who seem interesting, or as you are introduced to other people, remember that you have access to everything you have learned about being the life and soul of the party. You can hover with intention beside groups, build rapport wordlessly, enter conversations fluently and listen, listen, listen to your fellow partygoers ... but entertain them too when the moment's right. Practise this one more time in your imagination.

Be aware, in particular, of your smile. Think once more of the beliefs and resources it holds for you and allow it to welcome other people as they approach you. Let it give you the confidence to look others in the eye and to hold your own. Smiling is easy for you now. Let yourself smile at the people around you and allow yourself to feel the warmth of that smile being reflected back to you. Notice how that feels and hold that feeling for as long as you can, in whatever way is comfortable for you.

Maybe the group is talking about an area where your knowledge is not particularly great. But, as you continue to listen in your imagination, you notice that one of their keywords relates directly to something you saw as you prepared for this event. They smile encouragingly at you, for they are obviously as genuinely interested in hearing you as you are in communicating with them. Your opinion is valuable. So, as you make a comment on the subject, pitched at just the right level for the character of the party, you and these people, you can feel how much they have appreciated your words.

Hear yourself as you manage to tell a funny story about your day, or some recent occurrence that is absolutely and effortlessly relevant. Remember to use all your senses so that everyone is involved in your tale, including the sights and the smells. Perhaps you are amazed but proud and pleased to hear them giggling and laughing at your story. You now know that you can tell stories and even jokes that people really want to hear. You carry on as a part of their group, talking and listening, until there is a natural break and it is time to move on.

As you continue to imagine the event, someone to whom you might not have wanted to talk before, approaches. What will you have in common, you wonder? But as they begin their small talk, maybe about the weather or your journey, you realise that this is really a cry for help and that you have the tools to get this person to talk about what makes them feel really passionate about life. You catch some of this enthusiasm in just one of their keywords and gently lead them on to it. Then, you block out everything else that is happening and enter into the world of the person speaking to you. How do things look to them? What is the position of the concepts they are describing in the space around them? How much space do their ideas occupy? How might they feel, from the tone of their voice and the position of their body? In your imagination, you check back on your impressions of the person. They are delighted that someone has really listened to them and genuinely shared their enthusiasm. You are also astonished that you managed to find someone whom you would previously have thought of as dull, so interesting. You part on the best of terms.

You also mentally rehearse meeting the person or type of person that you have envisaged as part of this event. You are genuinely interested in their world and in what they have to say. In your imagination, if you have met them before, you find yourself easily and naturally recalling the details of your previous conversation. Because of this, you find that the two of you are getting on really well and the perfect opportunity arises for you to say something important. Be aware of how confident you feel as, boldly, you take the step you need. For example, you may need to request something. You make your request, confidently, clearly and politely. As it turns out, the person is pleased and flattered that you have asked, as well as, perhaps, impressed by your courage, so willingly agrees to help you in whatever way you need.

Very soon, food and drink may enter the scene, if they have not done so already. Find yourself doing everything you need in order to manage all of this efficiently, even as you are talking to people. This may include sitting down, if it feels right. As you sit down in your imagination, you are still feeling that you are very much part of the event, alert and open to its direction and nuances. This is reflected straight back to you when people voluntarily approach you and you begin to interact animatedly but considerately with them, just as you have previously with others.

As the event moves on in your mind, there may be other points that are of particular significance for you personally. As you move through them, you notice all the associated sights, sounds, feelings, smells and tastes. But, above all, you keep in mind how resourceful you are and how readily your new resources spring to your aid, just when you smile and access them.

As the time comes for you to leave, you gather together everything that you need and you realise just how well everything has gone. You know that there are matters left for you to tie up afterwards but that you can do so easily. You can also look back on the occasion with pride and pleasure, knowing that you will receive further opportunities and invitations as a result. Most of all, you are aware of how much you enjoyed yourself in whatever way that enjoyment manifests itself for you. You are genuinely grateful for having been able to meet so many interesting people and you are keenly anticipating the chance to attend your next social event so that you can build even further upon your now considerable skills. Maybe it has even inspired you to hold your own party or to move forward in some other way that's right for you.

Whatever the situation, allow yourself to revel in the new freedom that has opened up for you and to hold the feeling of pleasure as you anticipate the future. Hold that feeling for as long as you can before returning to the everyday world, knowing that you are the life and soul of the party, both inside and out.

Chapter Nine

Go!

If you can, before reading this last chapter, please go to a particular event or party for which you've prepared, as it will have more impact if you do.

You've done it. Allow yourself some time to bask in the warm glow of pleasure that comes from having been the real 'life and soul of the party' in your own most appropriate and genuine way.

Now it's time to use all the skills and knowledge you have gained to anchor these feelings into future events. Ideally, imagine yourself carrying them even more into the future, so that they are ready and waiting as a part of you next time that you need them. Maybe a particular tune was playing as you enjoyed yourself, or the clink of a glass will bring back the memory, or maybe just seeing someone else's smile will be enough to trigger those feelings of confidence whenever you need a boost.

Keep going, too

So, bask for as long as you like in these new sensations. You deserve it. You've gained a new skill and discovered even more about yourself in the process.

However, keep in mind from this point onwards that the 'life and soul' process continues. It doesn't just begin with deciding to go to an event and end the moment you head off home. Instead, it is an ongoing, spiralling, infinite progression.

To help your social life flourish (and you might as well as you've come this far), you need to maintain the relationships and contacts that you've begun to forge. Whether you chose to socialise at a parents' evening, an office party or your friend's birthday, your new-found skills will have got you noticed in the most positive way. Therefore, instead of simply melting into the background as you might previously have done, you have the opportunity to build up further connections. The question is, how?

The answer is outrageously simple. For every person whose card, telephone number or e-mail address you noted, for every promise that you made to 'keep in touch', 'meet for coffee' or 'visit your website', there is one strategy that will place you head and shoulders above anyone else in their eyes. Keep your promises. You'll be amazed at the effect this has on people. They will say things like, 'I didn't expect that you would actually call.' They will then remember both your sociability and your efficiency, a winning combination in today's world. They will automatically consider you to be reliable in addition to the positive impact you made initially. They will include you in their address books and, consequently, you will receive invitations and chances to attend even more events, meetings and other social opportunities. Your world will open up even further. In turn, this will give you the chance to socialise and party as your real self, with an ever-expanding group of people. And so the cycle goes on.

'What if people don't respond to me?' I hear you cry. Well, for a start, if you have offered to send information, make contact or whatever, you should do so, whether or not you receive a reply. If you contact others with the same enthusiasm with which you now party and have fun, I guarantee that you will certainly receive a positive response most of the time. As for anyone who doesn't contact you, well, they haven't read this book yet, have they? Concentrate your efforts and concern on those who do keep in touch.

Lasting friendships

If you continue to be the life and soul of parties and events for a period of time (and why wouldn't you?), it is virtually inevitable that you'll make more friends. Enough said, for most people but a small number who seek my advice and help in communicating their real selves, do seem to have a set of beliefs that prevents them from forming effective friendships after the party is over.

Their beliefs tend to run along the lines of:

'If I invite Bloggs to our event/my party and he meets Jones there, I'll then lose Jones as a friend/business contact because Bloggs is much more fun than me, so I can't risk them meeting.' Leaving aside that this person might need to read or re-read Chapter One of this book, they could change their mindset to something easier.

In fact, this person's assessment couldn't be further from what tends to happen. First, you can never guarantee how people will react to each other. Second, if Bloggs and Jones do like each other, then this can only be good news for you. As we saw at the very beginning, like tends to attract like. Therefore, if Bloggs meets someone at your event with whom they feel comfortable, he or she will also feel more comfortable about you, with thoughts like, 'Ah, we know the same sort of people'.

Moreover, even if they do form some kind of friendship or partnership, be it business or social, the situation can still give you a warm glow. One of my best friends met my husband's best mate at one of our parties and now they're married, so I can vouch for that 'glow' at first hand. In a business or friendship context, they may well also be more inclined to invite you to join in their plans. I have almost lost count of the opportunities that have come my way by this means. So, the message is – friendship works.

Have fun ... everywhere

So far, the emphasis has been very firmly on specific events at which you can have fun and these are varied enough, from an after-work drink, to a morning's roller-blading, from dinner parties to half an hour in the jacuzzi at your conference hotel.

However, what would it be like if the opportunities to spread some party spirit became even broader? You could be the life and soul of a chat at the bus-stop, if you want, or of any conversation, anywhere you choose, for that matter. If you keep up the idea of forever striking up conversations with people who might previously have been outside your sphere, you'll be astonished at how rich, exciting and varied your world will become.

And now, go on ...

Finally, give yourself an enormous reward right now. You've learnt a huge number of skills, initiated a vast amount of change and become the life and soul of any party that feels right to you. In fact, you now have much more than just a part of your life that has become more social. You have the skills, ideas and ability to put your real soul into your life, in whatever way you choose.

Only you will know how to use these ideas. You may apply them to beliefs that have held you back in the past about work, love, money, happiness or freedom. Or you might choose to share them with someone who's noticed the change in you and wants to know more.

However you choose to take things forward, thank you for reading this book. Whatever you do, stay in touch and, please, have fun.

Appendix 1

List of Activities

Introduction
What being the life and soul of the party means to you   8
Imagining yourself as the 'life and soul' of a party   11

Chapter One: It's All About Attitude
What are your beliefs about the idea of being the
'life and soul of the party'?   21
What would you like to believe?   22
Beginning your belief change   23

Chapter Two: Create Your Carrot
Emotional baggage clearance   33
Create that carrot   37

Chapter Three: Everything But the Words
Getting in step   41
Positive hovering   47
Joining a group   49
Be aware of your progress   55
Welcome to my world   57
Changing the face of boredom   61
Different angles   62
New conversations   64

Chapter Four: How to Talk About Anything
What interests you?	68
Linkups	70
Get a word in edgeways	71
Random talking	76

Chapter Five: Questions, Questions
Imaginative questions	79
Newscasters	82

Chapter Six: A Trip to the Theatre
Links	88
The random dozen	88
Making comparisons	95
True expression	98
Spot the anecdote	99
Story time	100

Chapter Seven: Get Ready …
Ideas for getting invites	111
Your party preferences	113
What feels right to you?	118
Positive associations	122
Resource yourself	124

Chapter Eight: Get Set …
Final mental rehearsal	131

Appendix 2

Conversation Starters

When you're starting conversations, the golden rule is that 'less is more'. The other person may well only be too happy to run off with the conversation at the slightest encouragement. Here are some ideas, if you feel you need them.

To begin a conversation

This is the stage of conversation where 'small talk' is appropriate and almost expected. So, routes into the conversation might include:

- Questions about the person's connection with the event you are attending.
- Comments about how you are enjoying the event (only if you are), finishing with a question about their enjoyment.
- Comments about the location (if positive).
- Comments about the weather (if it is genuinely remarkable at the time).
- Compliments (as long as they are genuine).

People sometimes ask whether they should say, 'Haven't I seen you somewhere before?'

There's no hard-and-fast rule but it's probably better to say this only if you really do mean it, to avoid it sounding like a corny chat-up line. The same goes for, 'Do you come here often?'.

To broaden a conversation

To help another person to talk in more general terms, use openings like:

- 'How are you?'
- 'What do you enjoy most about …?'
- 'If you could do anything right now, what would it be?'
- What drew you to …?'
- 'What would be your ideal job/holiday etc.?'
- 'Why?'

To help a person be more specific

Useful routes include:

- 'Hi. I'm [Bloggs]. What's your name?'
- 'What do you do?'
- 'Where are you from?'
- 'How should I go about [doing a particular task]?'
- 'Where do you live?'

Resource List

The books mentioned in the text are:

Phantoms in the Brain: Human Nature and the Architecture of the Mind, by V.S. Ramachandran with Sandra Blakeslee, Fourth Estate: London, 1998.

Mind Sculpture: Your Brain's Untapped Potential, by Professor Ian Robertson, Bantam: London, 1999.

Pride and Prejudice, by Jane Austen, Wordsworth Editions Limited: Ware, Hertfordshire, [1813] 1992.

For more information on different types of communication, try:

You Just Don't Understand: Women and Men in Conversation, by Deborah Tannen, Virago: London, 1991.

Dare to Connect: How to Create Trust, Confidence and Loving Relationships, by Susan Jeffers, Piatkus: London, 1992.

Flirt, by Peta Heskell, Thorsons: London, 2001.

If you would like more information about the theory underpinning this book and how to apply it yourself:

Books

The Elements of NLP, by Carol Harris, Element Books: Shaftesbury, 1998.

Principles of NLP, by Ian McDermott and Joseph O'Connor, Thorsons: London, 1996.

NLP at Work: The Difference that Makes a Difference in Business, by Sue Knight, Nicholas Brealey: London, 1995.

Websites

www.selfworks.net – Clare's own website. Get in touch here.

www.anglo-american.co.uk

www.crownhouse.co.uk

www.nlpanchorpoint.com

www.nlpu.com

www.nlp-community.com

For deeper, but nevertheless very enjoyable insights into social and other behaviour, try:

Changing Belief Systems with NLP, by Robert Dilts, Meta Publications: Capitola, CA, 1990.

The New Peoplemaking, by Virginia Satir, Science and Behaviour Books: Mountain View, CA, 1988.

Time Line Therapy and the Basis of Personality, by Tad James and Wyatt Woodsmall, Meta Publications: Cupertino, CA, 1988.

How to Win Friends and Influence People, by Dale Carnegie, Hutchinson, 1990.

Thank you for reading my book. If you have any feedback or would like more information, please e-mail me at any time at clare.walker@selfworks.net. As a reader of this book, you are entitled to a discount on Selfworks coaching or seminars. For further details, please contact me at the e-mail address above or visit my website www.selfworks.net.

Clare